Celebrating

—— the ——

Jewish Holidays

Life-Affirming Secular and Spiritual Observances

Valerie Toizer Bloom

Dedication

To my sons, Shiloh and Bodin, with love and gratitude.

As we hold our children in our arms and hearts,
we touch the past, the present, and the future.

Contents

Acknowledgements

It is with tremendous appreciation that I thank my family and friends who supported my efforts in writing this book. I would like to especially acknowledge Alfred Toizer, Elayne Toizer, Nicki Toizer, Edie Kligman, Linda Kligman, Ann Bluestein, and Dena Lake for their proofreading and feedback, and Rebecca Maki (rebecca1402@comcast.net) for the cover design.

1. An Invitation to Celebrate

T he annual cycle of Jewish holidays offers us a warm invitation to both connect with our cultural heritage and explore who we are today. While each holiday commemorates its own particular event, many of the holidays are interrelated, creating a year that is full of meaning as we celebrate life from a Jewish perspective.

There are certain themes that recur during the Jewish holiday cycle. These include agricultural and historical events, as well as dedicating and rededicating ourselves to our goals, to God, to our community, and to living in accordance with our values. The Jewish holidays abound with opportunities to celebrate nature, renew our spirits, practice self-awareness and self-improvement, help those less fortunate than ourselves, repair the world, and retell the ancient stories of the Jewish people.

Being Jewish is multifaceted. "Jewish" refers to both a cultural heritage and a religious belief system. Each of these can be further divided into various identities, traditions, and worldviews. Within these overlapping aspects of Judaism lies tremendous possibility and flexibility for you to choose how to express what Judaism means to you. You can decide which occasions to celebrate and how. Your celebrations can reflect religious or spiritual beliefs or be completely non-theist. This book is a resource to help you find ways of enjoying secular and spiritual celebrations of Jewish holidays and provides various ideas for holiday rituals. The rituals described in this book take place outside of the synagogue; they can stand alone or in tandem with religious services.

Reading this book and reflecting upon what is important to you and your family will help you identify which holiday celebrations you find compelling. Over time, your thoughts and feelings about the Jewish holidays may change, and the way you celebrate can reflect that. Judaism has been adapting for thousands of years, with people in each generation deciding how to express their beliefs and honor their culture. And now it is your turn to continue this rich tradition by exploring what Judaism means to you and how to celebrate its holidays. Judaism is strong enough and flexible enough to play a meaningful role in your life, whatever your religious beliefs and relationship to your cultural heritage are.

Adapting observances to reflect current understandings and interpretations of Jewish history, culture, and religious dogma allows Judaism to survive and thrive in modern times. The idea is to find beauty and meaning in the ancient traditions and to honor Jewish heritage in ways that complement our values and make sense to us. Those of us who are parents may want to transmit the Jewish culture to our children and teach them what it is to be Jewish in the framework of our own family's value system.

This book is intended to serve as a guide as you consider how you want to express your Jewish beliefs and culture. The history and meaning of each holiday are discussed. Some suggestions are made for how to celebrate each holiday, though these should not be considered exhaustive lists. Using your own experience and creativity, you can build upon the ideas found in this book to develop rituals that bring meaning and joy to your expression of Judaism.

Each person reading this book brings with them their own views about religion. You may consider the Torah (the first five books of the Bible) to be the literal word of God, the writings of ambitious rabbis, or a book of myths. You may have a traditional Jewish belief in God, envision God in another way, or identify as atheist or agnostic. Because those of you reading this book may have widely differing thoughts and feelings about God, I will leave it to you to interpret the word "God" in whatever way makes sense to you. My purpose in referring to God is not to promote a specific belief system but to put the Jewish holidays into their historical religious context.

In addition to divergent religious beliefs, there are also a variety of cultural and political traditions represented among the readers of this book. Our understanding of nature, agriculture, poverty, freedom, personal responsibility, and history depends upon our individual experiences and informs how we may interpret these common themes found in the Jewish holidays. We have differing thoughts about the modern State of Israel and its politics, which may color how we view the nature of Judaism. We have unique relationships with our families and friends, affecting how we celebrate different occasions in our lives.

Our perspectives on Judaism can be described as falling along a continuum, as opposed to fitting into precise categories. Individuals may consider themselves to be any combination of religious, spiritual, and cultural observers of Judaism. Whoever you are and whatever your beliefs, you will be able to find aspects of Jewish holiday celebrations that feel right to you and reflect who you are as a person.

Welcome to an exploration of the Jewish holidays and of ourselves!

2. Branches of Judaism

Judaism's two principal texts are the Torah and the Talmud. The Torah is comprised of the first five books of the Bible: Genesis, Exodus, Leviticus, Numbers, and Deuteronomy. Based on stories that had been orally transmitted for generations, it is believed that the content was first written down between the years 600 BCE and 400 BCE (Before Common Era). The Talmud, written between the years 200 CE and 500 CE (Common Era), is a collection of ancient rabbinic writings concerned with Jewish law and includes interpretations of the meaning of the Torah.

There is a strong tradition in Judaism of encouraging people to learn, question, discuss, and interpret the Torah and the Talmud in order to find personal understanding and meaning in one's beliefs. The Hebrew word *derash* ("interpretation") encompasses this ideal. We are expected to engage in the process of *derash* and come to our own conclusions concerning Judaism. In this model, the Torah may – and is allowed to – hold different meanings for different people.

It is helpful to have a basic understanding of some of the branches of Judaism in order to appreciate how the Torah and Talmud might be interpreted and incorporated into practice. The following are the more well-known movements, or denominations, of Judaism. You may or may not identify yourself as belonging to one of these movements; the brief descriptions are simply a way to help orient ourselves as we consider what Judaism means to us and how we want to celebrate the holidays on the Jewish calendar.

Orthodox: Orthodox Judaism is the most traditional branch of modern Judaism. Those in the Orthodox community observe a strict interpretation of *halakhah* (Jewish law based on the Torah and expanded upon in the Talmud) and believe that the Torah was written by God and given to Moses and the Israelites at Mount Sinai.

Hasidic: The modern Hasidic movement began in Poland in the 18th century under the guidance of Israel ben Eliezer, called the *Baal Shem Tov* ("Master of the Good Name"). The Hasidic branch focuses on the mystical expression of Judaism (*Kabbalah*), stressing the importance of joyful personal experiences with God more than religious education and ritual. Hasidim strive to find spiritual fulfillment in everyday activities.

Reform: The Reform movement was established in Germany in the early 1800s. It sought to meet the needs of many Jews who felt that the strict Orthodox traditions were too cumbersome for the more liberal political climate of the time. Reform Jews recited prayers in German rather than Hebrew, and they were not required to maintain kosher dietary laws. Some of the Reform rabbis denounced circumcision. (The ritual of circumcision continues to be actively debated among many Jews of different movements today.) The current Reform movement emphasizes ethics and action to improve the world. Some Reform congregations use gender-neutral language when referring to God.

Conservative: Founded in response to the Reform movement, Conservative Judaism bridges the gap between the Orthodox and Reform branches. It began in Germany in the 1840s and was introduced in the United States in the early 20th century. Conservative Judaism preserves traditions while providing less strict requirements than the Orthodox movement. Conservative Jews have widely varying personal beliefs regarding Judaism. Generally, members of Conservative synagogues believe the Torah was given to us by God but that it was written by people and thus has a component of human error and even corruption.

They see Jewish law as being adaptable and have borrowed elements from other cultures while remaining true to their belief in Judaism.

Reconstructionist: Reconstructionist congregations view Judaism as a combination of religious and cultural traditions that can change and grow. The movement adapts to contemporary society while honoring the history and values of Judaism. Reconstructionist synagogues always use gender-neutral language when referring to God. This branch of Judaism does not envision God as a personified deity who played an active role in historical events but rather as a force for goodness and compassion in the universe. If they choose to do so, individuals may accept *halakhah* as an important part of Jewish culture, with the belief that Jewish law was created by people and not by God. Reconstructionist Judaism grew out of the Conservative movement in the United States beginning in the 1920s and was established as its own branch in 1954.

Humanistic: Members of this movement, which is sometimes referred to as Secular Humanistic Judaism, strongly identify with Jewish history and culture but do not believe in God or any other supernatural being. As atheists or agnostics, they consider people to be solely responsible for their own lives. Non-theistic language is used in services, rituals, and celebrations, and particular attention is paid to the importance of equality and dignity for all people. This branch of Judaism was established in the United States in 1963 by a rabbi from the Reform movement.

Along with various theologies, there are also different Jewish heritages, the most common of which are Ashkenazic and Sephardic. These are not religious sects but rather ancestral lineages that lend some specific cultural traditions to our Jewish identities. Ashkenazim are descendants of Jews from Germany, France, and Eastern Europe and represent the vast majority of the world's Jewish population. Yiddish is the common language associated with Ashkenazic Jews. This language combines Hebrew and Aramaic with German. As the Ashkenazim moved into parts of Eastern Europe, Slavic languages were incorporated into local Yiddish dialects.

The second largest population is that of the Sephardic Jews, whose ancestors came from Spain and Portugal. Jews were expelled from the Iberian Peninsula in 1492 as part of the Spanish Inquisition. When they dispersed, many settled in North Africa and the Middle East. The common language spoken by the Sephardim is Ladino, a blend of Hebrew and Spanish.

The Mizrahi Jews have cultural practices that are very similar to those of the Sephardi Jews. The Mizrahim trace their ancestry back to the Jews who originally lived in Babylonia and remained in the area of the Middle East and North Africa throughout the centuries. The Mizrahim commonly speak Judeo-Arabic, combining Hebrew with the local Arabic dialect. There are a handful of smaller subsets of Jewish ancestral lineages, most of which are related to the Sephardim. This includes Oriental Jews – descendents of Sephardim who migrated to Asia.

3. Tikkun Olam

The concept of *tikkun olam* is deeply seated in Jewish faith and culture, though it has held different meanings for different people over the years. Literally translated as "world repair," *tikkun olam* in modern times primarily refers to working to improve society and is expressed by engaging in actions to promote social justice. We help the hungry, poor, and disadvantaged in order to make the world a better place. Traditional observances of various Jewish holidays include taking action to help repair the world, so specific opportunities for *tikkun olam* occur throughout the year.

We do not engage in *tikkun olam* simply to be kind and socially responsible. We do it because it is our duty, our obligation, our honor to help heal the world. Doing so connects us to a higher spiritual plane and fulfills part of our Covenant with God, that we have a shared responsibility to care for the earth and its inhabitants. There are two equally important aspects of *tikkun olam*: engaging in acts of kindness and making charitable donations.

Through *gemilut hasadim*, or acts of kindness, we take personal action in order to help repair the world. *Gemilut hasadim* can take many forms. Some examples include visiting those who are sick, lonely, in mourning, or otherwise struggling; volunteering at a local food bank; participating in beneficial community events; and lending a helping hand when there is an opportunity to do so (for instance, helping a neighbor to shovel snow in the winter). These acts of kindness can be done informally as we go about our daily activities, or they may be part of a specific group effort, perhaps being coordinated by a religious or community organization. Both adults and children can participate in these actions.

We help wealthy and poor alike through our acts of kindness, for everyone can benefit through the kindness of others. *Gemilut hasadim* is a powerful force, since it connects us through direct action to healing the world. It encourages us to build relationships, understand the struggles of others, and take personal responsibility for making the world a better place. It has often been said that we help ourselves in the act of helping others, so *gemilut hasadim* heals those who are taking action as well as those who are being assisted.

Tzedaka, or charitable giving, is the other major aspect of *tikkun olam*. Literally translated as "righteousness," *tzedaka* is not considered to be a voluntary act but an obligation. Indeed, even the poor among us are charged with the responsibility for helping others through charitable donations. *Tzedaka* does not have to take the form of a monetary contribution; it can be a donation of food, clothing, household items, or other goods. The Jewish holidays naturally lend themselves as occasions to make donations to relevant agencies. We may feel inspired to help the poor and hungry, aid those who are struggling against oppressive governments or injustice, assist people who are disadvantaged or hurting, or support the planting of trees, as we honor the meanings of the various holidays. By giving to appropriate agencies, we are helping to heal the world.

If you have children, they may be actively engaged in *tzedaka*. They may make financial or other contributions of their own or take part in family conversations about why donations are being made and which agencies to support. In this way, they can play a meaningful role in the process, and the charitable contribution is elevated to something much more than an adult quickly and quietly writing a check of financial support to an agency of their own choosing.

There are a multitude of worthy charities that operate in different ways. Donating to a local charity does the most good in your own community. But some charities, by their very nature, work best on national or international scales. Prior to giving to any charity, it is important to make sure it is a legitimate organization that does what it claims and uses donations to carry out its mission without allocating too much for salaries and operating costs. You can research agencies online through charity-rating sites such as charitywatch.org, charitynavigator.org, and greatnonprofits.org.

In addition to *gemilut hasadim* and *tzedaka*, many observant Jews also consider doing *mitzvot* (commandments from the Torah) to be a facet of *tikkun olam*. The belief is that by living devout and honorable lives as individuals, there is an aggregate positive effect on the larger society.

Engaging in *tikkun olam* is an expression of Jewish faith and culture. It is our way of making the world a better place for everyone, and the Jewish holidays offer perfect opportunities to do this.

4. Blessings

Reciting blessings has traditionally been an important ritual in Jewish life. Conscientiously reciting blessings helps us to express gratitude, elevate the moment to one of a more spiritual nature, and feel connected to our past and to the Jewish community. When a blessing (*b'rakhah* in Hebrew) is recited, everything else is still as we enter a state of serenity to commemorate the occasion.

It is for each person to determine for themselves what role reciting blessings should play in their celebrations of Jewish holidays. You may choose to recite blessings in the traditional manner or adapt them to better reflect your specific worldview. You may decide to incorporate certain blessings but not others, or you may choose to not recite any blessings at all.

Chanting (singing) the traditional blessings in Hebrew can inspire a powerful spiritual connection to our celebrations as it helps us to transition out of the mundane and focus on the moment. If you do not know the tunes that accompany the blessings or do not feel moved by the musical quality of the chant, you may recite the blessings in simple spoken form. (You can find examples of chanted blessings online.)

Whether chanted or spoken, blessings connect us to the past, knowing that countless others have uttered the same blessings through the centuries. They also unite us with the Jewish community of today, other members of which are reciting the same ancient words in their own homes or synagogues. If you, your family, or your guests do not understand Hebrew, it is a good idea to also recite the blessings in English. Or say them only in English if Hebrew holds no meaning or comfort for you.

Traditional Hebrew blessings give thanks to God and reference God as an all-powerful, omniscient, male entity. This reflects conventional Jewish religious dogma. If reciting such words causes discomfort because the religious imagery does not fit with your personal ideology, you may choose words that express the intent of the blessing in a way that feels right to you. As an example of the range of blessings that are used by different branches of Judaism, let us take a look at the blessing for bread, *ha-motzi*.

Traditional Ha-Motzi in Hebrew (transliterated)
Baruch Atah, Adonai Eloheinu, Melech ha-olam,
ha-motzi lehem min ha-aretz.

Traditional English Translation
Blessed are You, Lord our God, King of the universe,
who brings forth bread from the earth.

Reconstructionist Interpretation
Blessed are You, Holy One, life of all worlds,
who brings forth bread from the earth.

Humanistic Interpretation
Blessed are those who bring forth bread from the earth.

It is possible to bridge the gap between honoring both the ancient heritage and modern worldviews by reciting the traditional Hebrew blessing followed by a contemporary interpretation. Make sure to present the modern interpretation as such, rather than as a literal translation of the traditional blessing.

At the end of each holiday's chapter is a description of the traditional blessings that typically accompany that holiday. You can find more ideas for blessings by searching online or looking at a *siddur* (prayer book) for the branch of Judaism that best suits you. And, of course, you are free to use your own words to commemorate and celebrate various occasions.

5. The Jewish Calendar

The Jewish calendar is based on the cycles of both the moon and the sun. Originally, it was a lunar calendar, the months beginning with each new moon. Various festivals were celebrated on specific days of the lunar months. So, for example, the spring festival of Pesach was observed on the 15th day of the early spring moon. The *shofar* (an instrument made from the horn of a ram) was sounded in ancient Jerusalem when the first sliver of the new moon was observed. Fires were lit on hillsides to inform Jews in the surrounding areas of the beginning of the new month. Knowing when the new moon arrived was critical to ensure that festivals were celebrated on the correct days.

Each lunar month lasts for 29 or 30 days, since it takes the moon 29.5 days to travel around the earth. As the Jewish population spread to more distant lands, a tradition developed of celebrating the holidays for two days outside of the area of Jerusalem. This compensated for the uncertainty of whether a particular month was 29 or 30 days in duration, and the people could be confident that the holiday would fall during the time of their celebration. Today it is still common practice for Orthodox and Conservative Jews living outside of Israel to observe holidays for an additional day.

In ancient times the Temple in Jerusalem was central to Jewish life and holiday celebrations. The First Temple, built under the direction of

King Solomon in 957 BCE, was destroyed by the Babylonians in the year 586 BCE. Following the fall of the Babylonian Empire, construction of the Second Temple in Jerusalem began in 538 BCE, authorized by the new Persian king, Cyrus the Great. Like the First Temple, the Second Temple became the central site of worship for Jewish festivals and rituals. Many thousands of Jews would converge on the Temple during the pilgrimage festivals of Pesach, Shavuot, and Sukkot. In the year 70 CE, while Jerusalem was under control of the Romans, the Second Temple was destroyed. Following this event, many of the surviving Jews fled the region.

As a result of this Diaspora – the dispersion of the Jewish people away from the homeland – Jewish traditions were forced to evolve in order to survive. No longer could Jews rely on a single, central location as the focus of their religious lives and customs. Many changes took place, including an extraordinary update to the Jewish calendar.

Because the Jewish population was becoming increasingly scattered, it was critical to standardize the calendar and create a written version so that everyone would know when to observe the holidays. The lunar calendar created some confusion because it does not quite fit into the solar year. The twelve lunar months add up to 354 days. But since it takes the earth 365.25 days to circle the sun, basing the calendar on the lunar months would cause the timing of the holidays to "slip backward" over the years. The autumn harvest festival of Sukkot, for example, would arrive during summer, then spring, then winter, then back to autumn over the course of several decades. Because the Jewish holidays must be held at specific times of the year to correspond with agricultural and historical events, having them occur during the wrong seasons would be completely unacceptable. During Temple times, the authorities in Jerusalem could make rather informal adjustments to the calendar as necessary. But when the Jewish population dispersed to faraway lands, this was no longer a practical option, since locally made changes to the calendar could not be effectively communicated to all members of the Diaspora in a timely manner.

In the year 359 CE, under the direction of patriarch Hillel II, a 30-day leap month was incorporated into the lunar calendar in order to more effectively align it with the solar year. Consequently, the holidays would "slip" by only a matter of a few weeks before being adjusted by a leap month. The leap month is inserted before the last month of the calendar year seven times over a 19-year period, which is once every two or three years. When the leap month is added, it is called Adar. Since it is inserted before a month that is already called Adar, the "regular" Adar is called Adar II on leap years.

The Jewish Calendar

Month on the Jewish Calendar	Corresponding Month on the Civil Calendar	Holidays and Observances
1. Nisan	March/April	Pesach Holocaust Remembrance Day (Yom Ha-Shoah)
2. Iyar	April/May	Israel Independence Day Lag B'Omer Jerusalem Day
3. Sivan	May/June	Shavot
4. Tammuz	June/July	
5. Av	July/August	Tisha B'Av
6. Elul	August/September	
7. Tishri	September/October	Rosh Ha-Shanah Yom Kippur Sukkot Shemini Atzeret Simchat Torah
8. Heshvan	October/November	
9. Kislev	November/December	Hanukkah
10. Tivet	December/January	
11. Shevat	January/February	Tu B'Shevat
12. Adar	February/March	Purim
On Leap Years		
12. Adar I	February/March	
13. Adar II	March/April	Purim

Rosh Ha-Shanah, the Jewish new year, occurs during the early autumn month of Tishri, which is the seventh month on the Jewish calendar. The first month, Nisan, falls in early spring. This is because the first month of the year is based on pre-Israelite cultural traditions that considered the year to begin with the coming of spring. Indeed, our own civil calendar originally had March as the first month of the year. The name of the ninth month of September comes from the Latin root word *septem*, which means seven; the tenth month, October, comes from the root *octo*, meaning eight; the eleventh month, November, means nine, and December, the twelfth month, means ten. For the names of these months to align with their placement on the calendar, March – what is now the third month – would have to be the first month.

As you can see on the previous page, the months on the civil and Jewish calendars do not exactly align with each other but do fall within a range of several weeks – thanks to the Jewish calendar's leap month. The dates of the Jewish holidays, while consistent on the Jewish calendar, do move around a bit on the civil calendar. Hanukkah, for example, always begins on the 25th day of the month of Kislev on the Jewish calendar, while it predictably occurs during November or December on the civil calendar.

The Jewish calendar was designed to date the years from the time of creation, which was believed to be 3761 BCE. In order to calculate the year on the Jewish calendar, add 3760 to the year on the civil calendar. Add one more year if it is between Rosh Ha-Shanah – the Jewish new year – and December 31.

There is a striking difference between the Jewish and civil calendars in the way days are reckoned. On the Jewish calendar, each "day" begins at sundown. This means that the holidays begin on the previous evening for those of us who use the civil calendar. We have been taught that a day begins at midnight – so that when we wake up in the morning, it is a new day. According to the Jewish calendar, the new day arrives before we go to bed. This is because of the way days are described in the Book of Genesis in the story of creation: "There was evening and there was morning." The Jewish calendar carries with it the tradition of each day lasting from sundown to sundown.

The Jewish calendar is an incredible reflection of both lunar and solar time. Seasonal holidays are celebrated during the correct time of year, and the natural cycle of the moon is observed and honored. Having an accurate, predictable, written calendar enables Jewish people everywhere to know exactly when to celebrate the holidays.

6. Pesach

As winter releases its hold and we experience the rebirth of spring, we welcome Pesach. Commonly referred to as Passover, Pesach is the most ancient of the Jewish holidays. Its origins are found in spring festivals celebrated in pre-Judean societies. Over time, it became an agricultural festival, coinciding with the first of the grain harvests in the land of Israel. Following the destruction of the Second Temple in 70 CE, Pesach was transformed into a celebration of the Israelites' liberation from slavery under the Pharaoh in ancient Egypt, as described in the Book of Exodus. The three major themes of Pesach have some similarities and parallels: springtime, harvest, and liberation share images of rebirth, hope, gratitude, and life.

Pesach is the first of three pilgrimage festivals on the Jewish calendar, the other two being Shavuot and Sukkot. These three festivals honor the harvest cycles in the land of Israel. They are also related to each other Biblically, as they evolved from agricultural celebrations to commemorations of a sequence of stories in the Torah: the liberation from slavery in Egypt, the revelation of the Ten Commandments at Mount Sinai, and the ancient Israelites' 40-year journey through the desert in search of the Promised Land.

During the times of the First and Second Temples, adult men would travel to Jerusalem for the pilgrimage festivals to make offerings at the Temple altar. They would also give financial contributions to help maintain the Temple and provide for the sick and elderly of the community. The pilgrimage festivals helped to sustain Jewish culture. Separate tribes came together in ancient Jerusalem, identifying as Jews in a region that was populated by many pagan and idol-worshipping cultures. Pilgrimage festivals were opportunities for Jewish people to celebrate and learn together, reinforcing their faith and sense of community.

The Jewish calendar begins with the early spring month of Nisan, which corresponds to late March or early April on the civil calendar. Pesach is the first holiday of the Jewish year, beginning on the 15th day of Nisan and lasting for seven days in Israel and for Reform and Reconstructionist communities in the Diaspora. Conservative and Orthodox Jews in the Diaspora celebrate Pesach for eight days. This holiday is known by several other names, including *Hag Ha-Matzot* ("The Festival of Unleavened Bread"), *Hag Ha-Pesach* ("The Festival of the Paschal Lamb"), *Hag Ha-Aviv* ("The Festival of Spring"), and *Zeman Cheruteinu* ("Season of Our Freedom"). This wide variety of names reflects the complex history of the holiday.

Pesach is a highly ritualized holiday based primarily on telling the story of the Israelites' escape from the bondage of slavery in ancient Egypt. The quest for freedom was led by Moses, who followed instructions he received from God in a vision. According to the legend, Moses was born to a Jewish family and adopted into a royal Egyptian family. When he was a young man, he killed an Egyptian overseer who had been beating a Jewish slave. Having become an outcast because of this action, Moses fled to the desert, where he lived as a shepherd.

Years later, Moses had a vision of a bush that burned and yet was not consumed by the fire. In this vision, God told him to return to Egypt and tell the leader, Pharaoh, to free the Hebrew slaves. And so Moses met with Pharaoh and pleaded for his people, but Pharaoh refused to free them. God then sent a series of ten plagues to convince Pharaoh to release the Israelites from bondage. These plagues were blood (turning the water of the Nile River into blood), frogs, lice, beasts (flies), pestilence (cattle disease), boils, hail, locusts, darkness, and death of the firstborn. All of these plagues affected the Egyptians but not the

Israelites. Before the final plague, the Israelites were instructed to sacrifice lambs and use the lambs' blood to mark their doorposts. With this sign, the plague would "pass over" their homes, sparing the lives of their firstborn children while killing those of the Egyptians. Witnessing the horrors of the tenth plague, Pharaoh finally relented and set the slaves free.

The Israelites prepared to depart from the land of Egypt in great haste and left in what is known as the Exodus. Rather than taking the time to bake bread for their journey, they allowed the desert sun to quickly bake unleavened dough as they traveled. Because the dough, made only of flour and water, did not have time to rise, the resulting *matzah* formed a flat cracker.

After the Israelites departed, Pharaoh changed his mind and ordered his charioteers to capture the freed slaves and return them to bondage. The Israelites marched eastward until they came to the shore of the Red Sea. Behind them, Egyptian soldiers appeared, and the Israelites feared they were trapped. Miraculously, the waters of the Red Sea parted, and Moses and the Israelites crossed to the opposite shore. The soldiers pursued them, but the waters of the sea rushed back together, drowning the soldiers. Then began the Israelites' 40 years of traveling through the desert in search of the Promised Land of Canaan. Though there is quite a bit of debate regarding the details of the Exodus, this event is generally believed to have occurred around the year 1290 BCE.

Matzah (plural: *matzot*) is sometimes referred to as "the bread of affliction" or "the bread of poverty" and is a symbol of freedom for the Jewish people. The appearance of this bland, plain food on an otherwise elaborate Passover dinner table serves as a reminder that freedom should not be confused with wealth. Our sense of freedom is best connected to simplicity, and we must not allow ourselves to figuratively become slaves to material possessions. This simple bread of affliction is also the bread of redemption and can help to focus our attention on the bare essentials of freedom.

The *matzah* used for Pesach is made only of wheat flour and water, and not the varieties made with egg, salt, or other ingredients. Although *matzah* is produced and can be eaten throughout the year, there are special rules for making it kosher for Pesach. The strict baking process does not allow the flour time to rise whatsoever; it is completely unleavened bread. If a box of *matzah* is kosher for Pesach, it will be clearly labeled on the package.

While we traditionally consume *matzah* during Pesach, many Jewish people avoid *hametz*, or leavened grains, in observance of the holiday. These five grains are wheat, barley, spelt, rye, and oats. (Although made from wheat and water, kosher for Pesach *matzah* is completely unleavened and not considered *hametz*.) To this list of grains, Ashkenazic authorities have added rice and *kitniyot* (legumes): beans (including soybeans and soy products), peas, lentils, and millet. Some also consider peanuts to be *kitniyot*. The reason *kitniyot* were added to the list of foods not to be eaten during Pesach is that they can be ground into flour and leavened. Observant Ashkenazic Jews also avoid sesame seeds, sunflower seeds, corn (including corn syrup), vinegar (as well as all products with vinegar as an ingredient), baking powder, and liquors made from grains. (Many of these products can be made kosher for Pesach under the proper manufacturing conditions and with appropriate rabbinic supervision; kosher for Passover foods are all clearly labeled as such.) Sephardic Jews did not adopt the stricter guidelines and only avoid wheat, barley, spelt, rye, and oats during Pesach.

For Ashkenazic Jews, the list of what is considered *hametz* has grown longer over the years in order to ensure that there are no accidental violations of the diet indicated for Pesach in the Torah. In an effort to avoid unintentional mishaps, the rules have become quite cumbersome – to the point of being too extreme for some people who would otherwise be interested in observing Pesach's dietary restrictions.

There are those who feel strongly compelled to strictly avoid *hametz* during Pesach, while others are not drawn to the idea at all. The remainder have some level of interest but may be overwhelmed by the list of what is forbidden. Rather than feeling as if we must choose to do all or nothing, it is possible for individuals and families to find limited ways of exploring the prescribed diet of Pesach. For example, a person of Ashkenazic descent may feel that it is not necessary to avoid *kitniyot* because there is no realistic risk of the legumes being accidentally ground and leavened prior to being consumed. Other options include observing the dietary restrictions for a portion of the holiday rather than for the entire week, or strictly avoiding *hametz* only at dinnertime during Pesach.

For some people, the dietary laws of Pesach can feel overwhelming. However, the challenge of not consuming foods that we typically eat can also be extremely liberating, providing a meaningful expression to this holiday of freedom. We may not wear the shackles of slavery, but we are surely in the bonds of habit and routine. Doing something different, though it may be difficult and even intimidating, can infuse us with courage and strength. By the end of the holiday, we know that we are not slaves to our dietary habits and assumptions about food. We can use Pesach as an opportunity to challenge and re-examine our relationship with food, one of our basic needs for survival.

For those who do not consume *hametz* during the week of Pesach, there is a tradition of carefully and thoroughly cleaning the house – especially all parts of the kitchen – prior to Pesach in order to remove all *hametz* from the home. Some remove (or eat) every last crumb of *hametz*. Others carefully put *hametz* away to avoid accidentally eating it and may choose to tape a *hametz* pantry closed during Pesach. Those who are particularly observant will put away kitchen equipment, such as the food processor, that is used for *hametz* during the rest of the year. Some families have a second set of plates and silverware to be used only during Pesach, so that they remain uncontaminated by *hametz*. Items used throughout the year – including pots, pans, the refrigerator, and the oven – may be *kashered* (made kosher through ritual cleaning) in order to be used during the holiday.

On the day before Pesach, there is a tradition of performing a final search for *hametz*. Children especially enjoy this activity, using flashlights to search every nook and cranny in the home. A small amount of *hametz* should be left out for the children to find. Some people think of the removal of *hametz* from the home as symbolically removing evil and arrogance from within ourselves. We try to purify ourselves as we clean our homes in preparation for the holiday of liberation. Such a thorough cleaning of the home is a lot of work; this can be thought of as a small taste of the life of a slave and as a reminder that freedom only comes with great effort.

Many Jewish families help those in need through food donations at Pesach. Unopened packages containing *hametz* may be donated to those who are hungry and are not Jewish through churches, food pantries, or social service agencies. Kosher for Passover food can be given to Jewish people in need through synagogues or Jewish charities. Some people make it a point to donate to Jewish charities prior to Pesach, since kosher for Pesach foods can be rather expensive. These donations are part of *tikkun olam*, our shared responsibility to help repair the world.

The main event of Pesach is the *seder*, the ritual meal traditionally held after sunset on the first evening of the holiday. The word "*seder*" translates as "order" or "arrangement," and the order and arrangement of the *seder* conveys the story of the Jewish people's liberation from slavery in ancient Egypt. Rich with symbolism and storytelling, the *seder* is meant not only to teach the story of the Exodus but also to have participants feel as if they themselves have been personally liberated from the bonds of slavery. While there are certain aspects of the *seder* that are considered standard, there is plenty of room to be creative by incorporating songs, skits, poetry, artwork, discussion, games, or other features to make the *seder* your own. Be mindful of how long or short you want the *seder* to be when deciding what to include. The dining table may be adorned with flowers in celebration of spring, recognizing the most ancient aspect of the festival of Pesach.

The *seder* plate is the prominent feature of the dinner table. The plate itself can be either ornate or ordinary, and on it are displayed five symbols of Pesach:

karpas: A green vegetable representing spring and rebirth. This is often parsley, though celery, scallions, or lettuce may be used. The seder table also has small bowls of salt water (or lemon juice), in which to dip the *karpas*. The salty water symbolizes the tears of the slaves.

maror: Bitter herbs, usually horseradish, symbolizing the bitterness of slavery.

haroset: A mixture of chopped apples, nuts, and wine or grape juice that represents both the sweetness of freedom and the mortar used by the Israelite slaves to construct Pharaoh's buildings. The Sephardic version is a bit more sticky and spicy and features additional fruits, such as bananas and dates. The *haroset* lessens the bitterness of the *maror*, just as the promise of freedom can make it possible to endure slavery.

beitzah: A roasted egg recalling both springtime and ancient Temple sacrifices. (To roast an egg, hard-boil it and then put it on a stove burner or in a toaster oven until it becomes scorched and the shell begins to crack.) Vegans, who do not consume animal products, might substitute sunflower seeds, an avocado, or an edible flower for the egg.

z'roah: The roasted shank bone of a lamb to remember the sacrificial lambs in the story of the Exodus. Vegetarians can substitute a roasted beet, which gives the appearance of bleeding, or use a "paschal yam" instead.

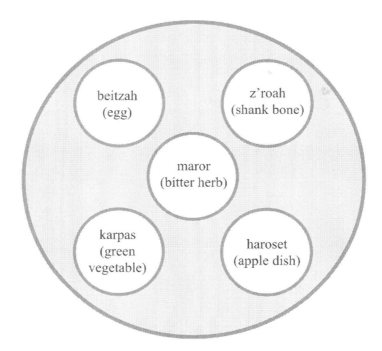

Common Arrangement of Symbols on the Seder Plate

Along with these five traditional items on the *seder* plate, an orange may be displayed to demonstrate support for the rights of gay, lesbian, bisexual, and transgendered people. Spitting out the orange seeds, we symbolically remove homophobia from ourselves and our communities. The metaphor of the orange can be expanded to include any person or group of people who are marginalized in society.

There can be one or two *seder* plates on the table, or each guest may have their own personal *seder* plate holding the items listed above. Next to the *seder* plate is a plate holding three special *matzot*. As with the *seder* plate, this can either be communal or individual plates. The three *matzot* are stacked on top of one another. You may use a special *matzot* cloth cover with three separate pockets or simply cover the *matzot* with a napkin.

Traditionally, the three *matzot* symbolize three classes of Jews: Kohen (priest), Levite (guardian of the Tabernacle, the portable temple used during the 40 years of travel through the desert), and Israelite (those who are not of the Kohen or Levite lineages). Today, it is more common for the *matzot* to represent those who are free but don't care (on the bottom), those who are not free (in the middle), and those who are free and care (the *matzah* on top).

During the *seder*, the middle *matzah* is broken into two halves, which may symbolize the breaking of the shackles of those who are not free. One half of this middle *matzah* becomes the *afikomen*, which is wrapped in a napkin or *matzah* cover and hidden somewhere in the house. After the Passover meal, the children search for the *afikomen* and may be awarded a small prize for finding it. The *seder* is not officially concluded until the *afikomen* is found and eaten, with each guest consuming a small portion of it. The half of the broken *matzah* that is not the *afikomen* may either be returned to the plate or passed around the table to create a symbolic shared meal as each guest breaks off a piece to eat.

The *matzot* on the table serve to remind us of the haste in which the Israelites fled Egypt and that freedom is for everyone – wealthy and poor alike. In addition to the three special *matzot* that are set aside, there are plates with *matzot* for guests to eat with the meal.

The *seder* has many components, making it necessary to have a special book to help guide us through the evening. The guidebook is called the *haggadah*, from the Hebrew word *hagged* ("to tell"), and it tells the story of Pesach. The story is told not only by describing the events of the Exodus, but also by encouraging questions and explaining the various symbols of Pesach.

More than 3,000 versions of the *haggadah* have been published, reflecting the incredible range of ways there are to tell the ancient story of the Exodus, relate the meaning of freedom, honor the struggle for liberation, and express our Jewish culture. As the wide variety of *haggadot* demonstrate, there is not a single "correct" manner in which to conduct the *seder*. You may select a published *haggadah* that expresses your worldview, or you may write your own *haggadah*, tailored to the needs of yourself, your family, and your guests.

The *haggadah* is meant to be read aloud, with each guest taking a turn, all guests reading in unison, or in some combination of these two. Each guest should have a copy of the *haggadah* so they can easily follow along with the readings. In retelling the story of the Exodus, those at the *seder* table should feel as if they themselves had been slaves, understanding that if they had not been liberated, then they and their descendents would continue to live in slavery. Indeed, this is our own story, as well as the story of the Israelite slaves.

Over the course of the *seder*, we are instructed to drink four cups of wine. The *seder*, however, is not intended to lead to drunkenness, and participants just take a small drink from their cups when the time comes to have the wine. Grape juice may be substituted for the wine, and people may also have a glass of any other beverage with their meal. If you are keeping kosher for Pesach, make sure that the wine has the appropriate label.

The times for having wine are indicated in the *haggadah* and are interspersed within the readings. The four cups of wine are strongly symbolic but may represent different ideas, depending on the nature of the *seder* itself. Traditionally, the four cups reflect the four aspects of redemption offered by God to the Jewish people: "I shall take you out of Egypt...I shall deliver you from slavery...I shall redeem you with a demonstration of my power...I shall take you as a nation." Non-traditional *haggadot* may indicate other interpretations of the four cups of wine, though they are always linked to the theme of the struggle for freedom.

A special cup of wine, typically an ornate goblet, may be set aside on the *seder* table. This is reserved for Elijah the Prophet who, it is said, will herald the arrival of the Messiah and the time of peace. But Elijah will not come until we ourselves have paved the way for peace. There is a beautiful Hasidic tradition in which all the guests at the *seder* table pour a bit of wine from their own cups into the cup for Elijah. In this way, they each contribute a little something to welcome the prophet and the time of peace. During the *seder*, a door to the house is left open so that Elijah may enter. In the Bible, Elijah is described in 1 Kings and 2 Kings as a man who stood up against immorality and idolatry under King Ahab, the ruler of the northern lands of Israel during the years of approximately 871-859 BCE.

Connecting ourselves and our guests to the experience of slavery during the *seder* may be encouraged through the readings and also through more interactive exercises. Guests can answer questions, imagining how they might have experienced slavery and liberation in the story of the Exodus. Perhaps guests can empathize with refugees today who must flee their homelands. Or there might be a discussion about our figurative enslavement to inner trappings such as habits of routine or material possessions. Guests may perform skits, sing songs, or create or present artwork to make the *seder* come alive for everyone.

Because we feel a strong personal connection to the experience of slavery during the Season of Our Freedom, we have an obligation to help those who are not free today. This obligation may be met through *tzedaka* (charitable giving) or *gemilut hasadim* (acts of kindness). Consider how people experience slavery and oppression today. What actions might be taken to help alleviate their suffering? We also have a responsibility to help the hungry. One traditional line of the *haggadah* is: "Let all who are hungry come and eat; let all who are in need come share our Passover." In times past, the poor were fed and helped directly by joining in another family's *seder*. Today, it may be more practical to donate money or volunteer time or resources to agencies – especially local agencies – that help to feed the poor.

Although Pesach is an occasion to specifically recall the Jews' liberation from slavery in ancient Egypt, it is also a natural opportunity to honor many other struggles for freedom. Pesach lends itself as a celebration of liberation, dignity, hope, and courage for all of humanity. The *haggadah* may incorporate descriptions or quotes about the Civil Rights Movement in the United States, the battle against Apartheid in South Africa, the Warsaw Uprising during World War II, modern political refugees and freedom fighters, and any number of other stories about the universal struggle for freedom in its various forms. You may want to include stories of freedom and liberation that are specific to the heritages or experiences represented by your guests, demonstrating the commonality of these themes. This helps to make the *seder* more relevant to them and offers the opportunity for everyone to learn more about each other's family and ancestral stories.

The purpose of identifying with the struggle for freedom of the ancient Israelites and others is not to feel as if we are victims or to become paranoid. Understanding and appreciating freedom from slavery ideally involves kindness and compassion toward others, even those who have enslaved us. In the Torah, the Jewish people are instructed to welcome others into their land (Lev 19:33, 34) and not to hate the Egyptians for having enslaved them (Deut 23:7). If we are consumed with hatred, we are not free. Freedom is not only a physical or political condition; it is also an emotional state.

Pesach is a family-oriented holiday, since the primary goal is to tell the story of the Exodus to the next generation. When planning your celebration, think about what kind of *seder* you and your guests want. Take into account everyone's needs, and do your best to make people feel included, bring the story of the Exodus to life, and have guests feel as if they have been personally liberated and redeemed. Encourage questions to be asked, particularly by children. It is a good idea to increase the feeling of involvement by having as many people as possible help with the *seder*. It is especially important for children to actively participate in order to help transmit the story to them.

The first and last days of Passover are the primary festival days. The intermediate days are considered "semiholidays," which don't carry all of the obligations and restrictions required by the Torah for "full holidays" (such as a prohibition from going to work). A *seder* may be held on any of the primary festival days. If you hold a second *seder*, that is a good opportunity to creatively expand upon the themes and activities of the first *seder*.

It is traditional to light festival candles on both the first and last days of Passover. The *shehecheyanu* blessing of gratitude is recited on the first day of Pesach, and a *yizkor* – a memorial candle for the deceased – is lit on the final day of Pesach.

There are many ways to be creative during Pesach, from designing the *seder* to trimming the dining table. The *matzot* and *afikomen* covers may be sewn, embroidered, or otherwise decorated; Elijah's cup may be ornately adorned; children are particularly enthralled with arts-and-crafts projects based on the ten plagues; images of springtime and freedom may be created for the occasion. Those who do not participate in a formal *seder* may, of course, contemplate the themes of Pesach on their own.

Pesach reminds us that even if we are born into slavery, we do not have to be destined to live our lives as slaves. Change is possible, and there is always hope for liberation. In the story of the Exodus, God redeemed us, but it is our responsibility to continue to strive for freedom – freedom for others as well as freedom from our own internal trappings. As springtime reveals a world of life around us, we are privileged to experience the rebirth of both nature and the human spirit.

Pesach: Blessings and Candle Lighting Information

Lighting the festival candles

On the first and last nights of Pesach, festival candles are lit. Some people light two candles, while others prefer to light one candle for each member of the family. (Please read Important Information about Candles on page 32.) Remember that the Jewish calendar marks days from sunset to sunset, meaning that on the civil calendar the holidays begin on the previous evening.

Blessing for lighting the festival candles

Baruch Atah, Adonai Eloheinu, Melech ha-olam,
asher kid'shanu b'mitzvotav v'tzivanu l'hadlik ner shel yom tov.

Blessed are You, Lord our God, King of the universe,
who has sanctified us with His commandments
and has commanded us to kindle the light of the festival day.

Blessing for lighting the festival candles on Shabbat
When the candles are lit on a Friday evening,
the blessing is slightly different.

Baruch Atah, Adonai Eloheinu, Melech ha-olam, asher kid'shanu
b'mitzvotav v'tzivanu l'hadlik ner shel Shabot v'shel yom tov.

Blessed are You, Lord our God, King of the universe,
who has sanctified us with His commandments
and has commanded us to kindle the light
of the Sabbath and the festival day.

Shehecheyanu: the blessing of gratitude
The *shehecheyanu* is recited only on the first night of Pesach.

Baruch Atah, Adonai Eloheinu, Melech ha-olam,
shehecheyanu v'kiyimanu v'higi'anu lazman hazeh.

Blessed are You, Lord our God, King of the universe,
who has granted us life, sustained us, and enabled us to reach this season.

Kiddush: the blessing for wine (or grape juice)
This is recited prior to drinking the first cup of wine
or grape juice at the *seder*.

Baruch Atah, Adonai Eloheinu, Melech ha-olam, borei p'ri hagafen.

Blessed are You, Lord Our God, King of the universe,
creator of the fruit of the vine.

Yizkor memorial candle

This candle, referred to as *yahrzeit* ("a year's time") in Yiddish, is lit in honor of loved ones who have passed away. It is traditionally lit on the last evening of Pesach. It is a good opportunity to think about your departed loved ones, and you may want to say a few words about them or recite a relevant poem or prayer. The *yizkor* ("remember") has enough wax to burn for a minimum of 24 hours and is traditionally lit on certain Jewish holidays as well as on the anniversary of the loved one's death. *Yizkor* memorial candles are lit as a cultural custom rather than as a traditional religious obligation, so they may take any form and be lit in whatever manner is meaningful to you.

Important Information about Candles

While festival candles are typically depicted as plain white tapers, the official guidelines for candles used in Jewish observances specify only that they should burn cleanly and with a fairly stable flame. Candles may be made of any material, may be any shape or color, and may even be scented.

Plant-based wax (such as soy or palm) or beeswax are non-toxic alternatives to paraffin wax and burn much more cleanly. Using oil candles is also an option, and plant-based oils (such as olive oil or canola oil) may be used in oil candles – but please consult the manufacturer's instructions before making a substitution with the fuel used. For those who choose to light scented candles, plant-based essential oils are a natural alternative to chemical-based fragrance oils. At this time, there are no all-natural dyes used to color candles.

Making your own candles can be a fun and meaningful project. There are supplies and kits for sale to make your own plant-based wax or beeswax candles, and there are instructions online for making oil candles at home.

7. Recently Established Holidays

In between the ancient holidays of Passover and Shavuot are several recently-established observances: Holocaust Remembrance Day, Israel Independence Day, and Jerusalem Day. These have all been declared official holidays by the Israeli Knesset (Parliament).

Holocaust Remembrance Day (Yom Ha-Shoah) is observed on the 27th day of Nisan in Israel and on April 19th in the Diaspora. It is a solemn day to honor the six million Jews who were killed in the Holocaust at the hands of Adolf Hitler's Nazi Germany. It is also a time to honor those who survived, as well as those who risked their lives to help the Jewish people in Europe. Remembering and trying to understand this dark period in history is an important obligation for all of us as civilized people. Observations for Yom Ha-Shoah are evolving as people struggle with how to commemorate events of such overwhelming horror and magnitude.

Yom Ha-Shoah translates as "the Day of the Total Destruction." Two-thirds of European Jews were killed in this genocide. The Holocaust ("burnt sacrifice") challenges traditional beliefs about divine justice and of God being the compassionate and all-powerful protector of the Jewish people. With the events of the Holocaust, we are confronted with the idea that God may choose to not intervene on our behalf, may not be able to control events, or may not exist at all. Many survivors of the Holocaust remained firm in their belief in God; others did not. Yom

Ha-Shoah differs from other Jewish holidays in its inherent questioning of the nature of God.

The atrocities of the Holocaust are beyond words; thus, many of the developing traditions involve periods of silence in an attempt to reflect the enormity of it all. There is a medieval Kabbalist custom called *tzom shtikah*, which is a fast of silence (as opposed to a fast from food) that has resonance during Yom Ha-Shoah observances. Silence not only gives us the opportunity to reflect on our personal thoughts and feelings, it also symbolizes the silence of the world community and of God during the Holocaust.

Yom Ha-Shoah observances in synagogues and other Jewish communities may include live or recorded testimonials from survivors; readings from authors such as Viktor Frankl, Elie Wiesel, Anne Frank, and others; reading the names of some of the victims; lighting candles; and singing songs. Words and sounds are often separated by periods of silence. Special programs are usually offered by Jewish and Holocaust museums on this day.

Many people honor the victims of the Holocaust by lighting *yizkor* memorial candles and reciting the *kaddish*, a prayer for the deceased. A tradition has emerged of lighting six of these candles, one for each million Jews killed in the Holocaust. Some people light a seventh memorial candle in honor of the Gentiles who were killed and of those who helped to save Jewish lives.

Homes may be decorated with yellow tulips, symbolizing spring and rebirth and also honoring the Netherlands, where a number of people worked to save Jewish lives during World War II. Some display a yellow Star of David, evoking the image of Jewish people being exposed and persecuted under Nazi rule when they were forced to wear a yellow Star of David on their clothing. A tradition has evolved in some communities of singing songs of hope and resistance. One example is "Hymn of the Partisans," a Yiddish song that was sung in ghettos and concentration camps.

Over time, some of the traditions for Yom Ha-Shoah will change. As survivors of the Holocaust pass on, the opportunity to meet with them personally will disappear. Fortunately, there are many video recordings of survivors, so their individual and collective stories will continue to inform and move future generations.

While it isn't specifically a Jewish holiday, there is another day set aside to remember and honor the victims of the Holocaust. International Holocaust Remembrance Day is observed on the 27th of January, the date on which the Auschwitz concentration camp was liberated in 1945. The United Nations General Assembly established International Holocaust Remembrance Day through a resolution in 2005.

Israel Independence Day (Yom Ha-Atzmaut) is celebrated on the 5th day of Iyar, which is usually in late April or early May on the civil calendar. Commemorating the War of Independence and the founding of the modern State of Israel on May 14, 1948, Israel Independence Day represents a return to the homeland for many Jews. Following their eviction from the land of Israel by the Romans in 70 CE, the Jewish people were without a home country and without government protection for nearly 1,900 years. While Jews were welcomed in some countries, at least for certain periods of time, they were frequently the target of hate and suspicion, blamed for various problems, and subjected to prejudice and persecution. Yom Ha-Atzmaut celebrates the birth of the country of Israel as well as the spirit of the Jewish people, filled with hope and determination.

In the United States, Israel Independence Day is celebrated in some cities and towns, where people enjoy parades and eat falafel and other foods from Israel. However, honoring the State of Israel is not entirely simple and straightforward for a number of Jewish people, who may have mixed feelings stemming from Israel's politics and its role in the Middle East. Israel Independence Day offers a wonderful opportunity for people to reflect upon what Israel means to them and how they feel about Israel's politics. It is important to consider Israel both in terms of its role as a political entity and as the homeland for the Jewish people; in this way, individuals can more fully explore their personal understanding of Israel.

Jerusalem Day (Yom Yerushalayim) is generally observed only in Israel as a kind of Memorial Day. Falling on the 28th day of Iyar, it commemorates Israel's capture of East Jerusalem from Jordan during the Six-Day War of 1967, which was fought against Syria, Egypt, Jordan, and Iraq. The Six-Day War occurred in early June on the civil calendar, and Jerusalem Day is celebrated shortly before the actual anniversary of the war.

The reunification of Jerusalem gave the Jewish people open access to the old city, including the ancient Western Wall of the Temple, for the first time since 70 CE. (Israel also captured the Sinai, the Golan Heights, and the West Bank as a result of this war.) In honor of Jerusalem Day, you might like to learn more about the city and its history, consider its role in historical and modern times, and think about what Jerusalem means to you.

8. The Omer

Seven weeks after Pesach, we celebrate Shavuot. These two holidays are connected on the calendar by the Omer ("a measure"), which lasts for 49 days, starting on the second day of Pesach. Shavuot occurs 50 days after the counting of the Omer begins. While the Omer itself isn't a holiday, this period of time has bearing on the Jewish holiday cycle.

An *omer* is a measurement of grain. During Temple times, an offering of the first grains of the new harvest was brought to the Temple in Jerusalem on the 16th day of Nisan, which is the second day of Pesach. At that time, the first sheaf of newly-harvested barley was ceremoniously waved in front of the Temple altar. The harvesting of grain crops continued through the Omer period, culminating with Shavuot, when an offering of two loaves of bread from that season's harvest was made at the Temple. (Shavuot is discussed in detail in the following chapter.)

In ancient times the Omer period was marked by prayers for favorable weather conditions as the crops grew; a poor harvest could have dire consequences for a community. For observant Jews today, the Omer continues to be a solemn time, one of "limited mourning," during which no wedding ceremonies take place.

The Omer is used by some as a time to prepare for Shavuot. While the holiday of Shavuot was originally celebrated as an agricultural festival, it evolved to become a commemoration of the giving of the Ten

Commandments and the Torah at Mount Sinai. Over the years, a Kabbalist tradition developed to help prepare oneself during the Omer to figuratively receive the Torah on Shavuot. In this custom, people reflect upon the various combinations of seven *sefirot* ("divine qualities") – one for each week of the Omer. Meditating upon these seven *sefirot*, people try to purify and elevate themselves to receive the law of God. By combining the following components, often referred to as emanations, we can explore fascinating aspects of psychology and behavior – in relation to the nature of God, human nature in general, and our own personalities in particular.

The seven *sefirot* can be described as loving-kindness (benevolence and compassion), strength (judgment and punishment), beauty (balances loving-kindness and strength), perseverance (grace), humility (submission), foundation (balances perseverance and humility), and majesty ("divine presence" that reflects all of the other *sefirot*). During the Omer, each day is used to consider how a particular *sefirah* might manifest itself within that week's theme. It may feel overwhelming to focus on combinations of *sefirot* every day for 49 days. If that is the case, you may choose to just think about one *sefirah* each week.

In addition to meditating upon these seven *sefirot*, you might use this time of the harvest season in the land of Israel to ponder the status of food and hunger around the world. Contrast the status of those in need with those individuals or countries having an overabundance of food. Consider making a donation to an agency that focuses on hunger relief efforts. You might also volunteer time at a food bank, collect food for the needy, or bring a meal to someone who could use it.

A minor holiday called Lag B'Omer occurs during the Omer. Literally translated as "33rd Day of the Omer," it falls on the 18th day of the month of Iyar. Lag B'Omer commemorates several Jewish heroes of the second century – Simeon bar Kochba, Simeon bar Yochai, and Rabbi Akiba.

Simeon bar Kochba led battles against the occupying Roman forces in the land of Israel. Though the rebellion was ultimately suppressed, Simeon bar Kochba is credited with being an effective commander in the resistance, capturing Jerusalem on Lag B'Omer.

The Seven Sefirot Examined During the Omer

	Day 1: Loving-kindness	Day 2: Strength	Day 3: Beauty	Day 4: Perseverance	Day 5: Humility	Day 6: Foundation	Day 7: Majesty
Week 1: Loving-kindness	Loving-kindness in Loving-kindness	Strength in Loving-kindness	Beauty in Loving-kindness	Perseverance in Loving-kindness	Humility in Loving-kindness	Foundation in Loving-kindness	Majesty in Loving-kindness
Week 2: Strength	Loving-kindness in Strength	Strength in Strength	Beauty in Strength	Perseverance in Strength	Humility in Strength	Foundation in Strength	Majesty in Strength
Week 3: Beauty	Loving-kindness in Beauty	Strength in Beauty	Beauty in Beauty	Perseverance in Beauty	Humility in Beauty	Foundation in Beauty	Majesty in Beauty
Week 4: Perseverance	Loving-kindness in Perseverance	Strength in Perseverance	Beauty in Perseverance	Perseverance in Perseverance	Humility in Perseverance	Foundation in Perseverance	Majesty in Perseverance
Week 5: Humility	Loving-kindness in Humility	Strength in Humility	Beauty in Humility	Perseverance in Humility	Humility in Humility	Foundation in Humility	Majesty in Humility
Week 6: Foundation	Loving-kindness in Foundation	Strength in Foundation	Beauty in Foundation	Perseverance in Foundation	Humility in Foundation	Foundation in Foundation	Majesty in Foundation
Week 7: Majesty	Loving-kindness in Majesty	Strength in Majesty	Beauty in Majesty	Perseverance in Majesty	Humility in Majesty	Foundation in Majesty	Majesty in Majesty

Simeon bar Yochai taught the Torah to numerous students, though doing so was punishable by death under Roman rule. His teachings became the foundation of the Zohar, the original text of Jewish mysticism. It is said that Simeon bar Yochai died on Lag B'Omer.

Rabbi Akiba was a second century sage, and numerous students of his were said to have died of a devastating plague. Legend has it that on Lag B'Omer the deaths from the plague ceased.

In honor of Lag B'Omer, you could learn more about these heroes or other heroes from Jewish history. On this day, the mourning of the Omer period is suspended, and weddings are permitted to take place. In Israel, Lag B'Omer is typically celebrated with picnics.

9. Shavuot

Shavuot, which literally means "weeks," is celebrated seven weeks after Pesach. As described in the previous chapter, Pesach and Shavuot are connected on the calendar by the Omer, a period of time marking the spring and summer harvests. Because farmers were busy harvesting both grain and fruit crops at the time of Shavuot, fewer people were able to make the pilgrimage to the Temple in ancient Jerusalem for this holiday than for the other two pilgrimage festivals, Pesach and Sukkot.

Shavuot is on the 6th day of Sivan, falling in May or June on the civil calendar. It is celebrated for one day in Israel and by Reform and Reconstructionist Jews in the Diaspora, and for two days by Conservative and Orthodox Jews in the Diaspora. At the time of Shavuot, the wheat harvest (the final grain harvest) begins in the land of Israel, and the first fruits of summer are ready to be picked. Fruits traditionally grown in Israel include grapes, figs, pomegranates, olives, and dates. Shavuot is also known as *Hag Ha-Katzir* ("The Festival of the Harvest") and *Yom Ha-Bikkurim* ("The Day of the First Fruits").

During Temple times, people brought offerings of the harvest to the Temple altar on Shavuot. Along with unprocessed grains and fruits, two loaves of bread made from that season's harvest would be offered. As the fruit harvest continued through the summer, people brought additional fruits to the Temple. Prayers of thanks were given for the harvest, and

God's continued blessings were also asked for successful future harvests.

With the destruction of the Second Temple in 70 CE, Jews could no longer bring offerings to their holy place in Jerusalem. Over time, as the Jewish people adapted their traditions to accommodate life in the Diaspora, less emphasis was placed on the agricultural origins of Shavuot, and the holiday became increasingly associated with the giving of the Ten Commandments on Mount Sinai. According to the traditional story, the Ten Commandments and the Torah were revealed to Moses on Mount Sinai during the month of Sivan, shortly after the Israelites fled slavery in Egypt. However, there is no connection made in the Bible between Shavuot and Moses receiving the Ten Commandments; Shavuot is referred to in the Bible only in terms of an agricultural festival.

The Book of Exodus describes both the Israelites' political liberation from Egypt (celebrated during Pesach) and the spiritual revelation at Mount Sinai (celebrated on Shavuot). While Pesach honors freedom, Shavuot defines the nature of that freedom as living in accordance with laws and serving God, the liberator. In this way, Shavuot can be seen as the sequel to the story of Pesach. Some may see a paradox within these stories. It may appear that the Israelites forfeited their newfound freedom in order to obey a new master – God. But within the confines of Jewish law, they experienced a tremendous sense of freedom and joy. Accepting laws by which to live allows people to thrive in civilized society, and complements (rather than conflicts with) freedom.

The commemoration of the giving of the Ten Commandments on Mount Sinai lends yet another name to Shavuot: *Zeman Matan Torateinu*, "The Season of the Giving of Our Law." The Torah describes the Israelites arriving at the base of Mount Sinai not long after leaving Egypt. Moses climbed Mount Sinai and returned 40 days later, carrying tablets inscribed with the Ten Commandments – the law by which the Jewish people would live.

It is important to note that, although we commonly refer to the "Ten Commandments," there are many people who consider God to have given us a total of 613 Commandments. Maimonides, a well-known Jewish philosopher of the 12th century, compiled a list of these

Commandments through his readings of the Torah. There are 248 "positive" Commandments described in the Torah – things we should do – and 365 "negative" Commandments – actions we should avoid doing. A number of these laws refer to animal sacrifices and other activities related to the Temple in ancient Jerusalem and are no longer applicable. Many other laws are considered out-of-date and are not observed, such as the requirement of a childless widow to marry her deceased husband's brother. There are quite a few commandments, though, stipulating ethical behaviors that are perfectly relevant in modern times, such as paying workers in a timely fashion and not committing fraud.

According to legend, the ancient Israelites were ill-prepared to receive the Torah at Mount Sinai. They trembled with fear when they heard God's voice as He started to enumerate the Ten Commandments. Rather than listening to God directly, they begged Moses to ascend Mount Sinai alone and speak with God, then return to tell them what God's wishes were. During Moses's absence, many of the Israelites engaged in idolatry, worshipping a golden calf of their own creation. When Moses returned with the Ten Commandments, he found the Israelites sleeping late rather than preparing themselves to receive the law of God. In his anger, Moses threw down the tablets with the Ten Commandments, breaking them into pieces. He then had to ascend Mount Sinai again in order to prepare replacement tablets.

There are a number of opinions regarding the revelation of the Torah by God to Moses. Some believe that the Torah – at least until the description of the Israelites' travels in the desert – was revealed to Moses and transcribed on Mount Sinai. Others believe that the Torah was revealed in segments. There is disagreement as to whether Moses or other scribes wrote down the words of the Torah promptly or over the course of the 40 years of wandering through the desert. And there are also those who do not believe this story is anything more than a myth, created and written many, many years after the events that it describes.

Whatever their precise origin, the Ten Commandments and the Torah constitute the basis of Jewish law. They outline a code of conduct that the Jewish people had to accept in order to enter into the Covenant with God, as described in the Bible. In this Covenant, which is frequently portrayed as the marriage between God and the Israelites, God and the Jewish people enter into a symbiotic relationship, working together to create a better world. In exchange for deliverance and redemption, the Jewish people agree to live according to God's laws, as outlined in the Ten Commandments and the Torah. The Ten Commandments indicate that we should live peacefully and honorably with each other, and this is how we are expected to conduct ourselves in life.

Here are the Ten Commandments, in simple language:
- Do not worship any other gods.
- Do not worship idols; worship God only.
- Use God's name with respect.
- Observe the Sabbath.
- Respect your parents.
- Do not murder.
- Do not commit adultery.
- Do not steal.
- Do not tell lies about others.
- Do not be jealous of others.

Although the Covenant with God is to be entered into freely, many of the ancient Israelites appeared to be terrified and therefore may have felt forced into accepting this arrangement. Today, Shavuot can be seen as an opportunity for us as individuals to understand what the Covenant means to us and to enter into it or reaffirm our commitment to it if we choose to do so. Many Reform synagogues hold *bar mitzvah*, *bat mitzvah*, and confirmation ceremonies on Shavuot, adding symbolism to the events as their members demonstrate a commitment to follow Jewish law, study the Torah, or enter into the Covenant with God.

Shavuot is the perfect time to think about and discuss the Ten Commandments. What do the Ten Commandments mean to you? How do they translate into today's society or into your personal life? What is the significance of the ancient Israelites entering into the Covenant by accepting the Ten Commandments as law? Would you have willingly entered into the Covenant had you been present during the legendary events at Mount Sinai?

We may also think about what the Torah as a whole means to us. Among the many beliefs regarding the Torah's origins are that it is the exact word of God, that it was transcribed with human errors and therefore not a precise record of God's words, and that it was created by ambitious rabbis who desired power and influence and is not the word of God at all. The Torah may be taken literally or as a book of myths, as historical fact, historical fiction, or a set of stories written to illustrate a system of beliefs. The Torah has been interpreted and reinterpreted countless ways throughout the centuries. What are your thoughts about the Torah? Do you want to make any particular commitment to reading the Torah or learning more about it?

The Season of the Giving of Our Law is also an ideal occasion to consider the importance of laws for civil society, as well as codes of conduct and principles by which we want to live our lives. Some individuals or families write their own additional "Commandments" on Shavuot. These can include anything from being polite ("Thou shalt say 'please' and 'thank you'") to refraining from taking on too many commitments ("I am allowed to decline when someone asks for a favor").

Homes, as well as synagogues, may be decorated with flowers, plants, and greenery for Shavuot. This celebrates the natural world of late spring and early summer. It also represents the trees and grass said to have grown at the base of Mount Sinai. Roses may be specifically chosen to adorn the home, recalling a legend that when the Israelites fainted from fear and awe upon hearing God's voice, He revived them with the smell of roses and spices. Paper flowers may also be used as ornaments. Some people go on a nature walk and take pictures of wildflowers to create a Shavuot collage, or cut actual flowers from their gardens to display as a table centerpiece.

Foods associated with Shavuot include fresh fruits that are just coming into season. While these can be found in your local supermarket, you might enjoy the experience of going to a pick-your-own farm to gather the fruits yourself, taking an active role in the harvest. (Fruits grown in more temperate climates may not be ripe for picking at that time of year.) Another option is to eat some of the fruits grown in the land of Israel, such as grapes, figs, pomegranates, dates, and olives. On Shavuot, *challah* (bread) is typically served as two oval loaves that are connected on a long side to resemble the two tablets of the Ten Commandments. They also symbolize the two loaves of bread presented as an offering at the Temple altar in ancient times.

There is a tradition of consuming dairy foods and honey on Shavuot, symbolizing the Promised Land of milk and honey and the image of the Torah as the book of milk and honey. It has also been said that dairy foods were consumed by the Israelites at the time of the revelation on Mount Sinai because the rules for kosher dietary laws regarding meat had not yet been written down. Rather than risk consuming meat that wasn't kosher, the Israelites ate vegetarian foods. These days we enjoy standard or vegan versions of cheesecakes, cheese *blintzes* (thin pancakes with filling), *bourekas* (stuffed pastries), *knishes* (stuffed, flaky pastries), or other dairy foods.

Festival candles are lit to usher in Shavuot, and a memorial candle for the deceased is traditionally lit. The *shehecheyanu* blessing of gratitude and the blessing over wine and bread are customarily recited.

In honor of the Israelites living in tents at the foot of Mount Sinai, some families celebrate Shavuot by camping, either outdoors or inside their homes. Fun can be had by designing meals around the image of Mount Sinai. For example, you could create a mashed potato Mount Sinai with broccoli trees at the base and carrot sticks to represent the Israelites. Or cupcake "mountains" with graham crackers, mini chocolate bars, cookie wafers or other "Ten Commandment tablets" standing on the top.

There is an Ashkenazic tradition of reading the Book of Ruth on Shavuot. Ruth was a Moabite woman who lovingly accepted the Jewish faith of her mother-in-law, making this an excellent story to demonstrate entering into the Covenant of Jewish law. King David, a descendent of Ruth, is said to have both been born on and died on Shavuot. Some people have a custom of reading from the Book of Psalms, which was written by King David and expresses mystical aspects of the Covenant with God. Shavuot may be used as an opportunity to study the Torah or to read the Ten Commandments aloud.

Originally an agricultural festival, Shavuot evolved into a commemoration of the giving of the Ten Commandments and the Torah on Mount Sinai. Shavuot is a special day for us to intentionally reconnect with nature, our food, the Covenant with God, the importance of laws in society, and our personal concepts of proper and honorable behavior.

Shavuot: Blessings and Candle Lighting Information

Lighting the festival candles

On Shavuot, festival candles are lit at sundown to usher in the holiday. Some people light two candles, while others prefer to light one candle for each member of the family. (Please read Important Information about Candles on page 32.) Remember that the Jewish calendar marks days from sunset to sunset, meaning that on the civil calendar the holidays begin on the previous evening.

Blessing for lighting the festival candles

Baruch Atah, Adonai Eloheinu, Melech ha-olam,
asher kid'shanu b'mitzvotav v'tzivanu l'hadlik ner shel yom tov.

Blessed are You, Lord our God, King of the universe,
who has sanctified us with His commandments
and has commanded us to kindle the light of the festival day.

Blessing for lighting the festival candles on Shabbat

When the candles are lit on a Friday evening,
the blessing is slightly different.

Baruch Atah, Adonai Eloheinu, Melech ha-olam, asher kid'shanu
b'mitzvotav v'tzivanu l'hadlik ner shel Shabot v'shel yom tov.

Blessed are You, Lord our God, King of the universe,
who has sanctified us with His commandments
and has commanded us to kindle the light
of the Sabbath and the festival day.

Shehecheyanu: the blessing of gratitude

Baruch Atah, Adonai Eloheinu, Melech ha-olam,
shehecheyanu v'kiyimanu v'higi'anu lazman hazeh.

Blessed are You, Lord our God, King of the universe, who has granted us life, sustained us, and enabled us to reach this season.

Kiddush: the blessing for wine (or grape juice)

Baruch Atah, Adonai Eloheinu, Melech ha-olam, borei p'ri hagafen.

Blessed are You, Lord Our God, King of the universe, creator of the fruit of the vine.

Ha-Motzi: the blessing for bread

Baruch Atah, Adonai Eloheinu, Melech ha-olam,
ha-motzi lehem min ha-aretz.

Blessed are You, Lord our God, King of the universe, who brings forth bread from the earth.

Yizkor memorial candle

This candle, referred to as *yahrzeit* ("a year's time") in Yiddish, is lit in honor of loved ones who have passed away. It may be lit on Shavuot. It is a good opportunity to think about your departed loved ones, and you may want to say a few words about them or recite a relevant poem or prayer. The *yizkor* ("remember") has enough wax to burn for a minimum of 24 hours and is traditionally lit on certain Jewish holidays as well as on the anniversary of the loved one's death. *Yizkor* memorial candles are lit as a cultural custom rather than as a traditional religious obligation, so they may take any form and be lit in whatever manner is meaningful to you.

10. Tisha B'Av

During July or August on the civil calendar is a Jewish holiday that gets little attention in non-Orthodox communities in modern times. Tisha B'Av – literally "9th of Av," the date on which the holiday falls – is a day of mourning. On it we remember the destruction of the First Temple in 586 BCE and the Second Temple in 70 CE, both of which are said to have occurred on the 9th day of Av. At the time of the destruction of each of these Temples, many Jews were killed and many more exiled from their homeland.

While the destruction of the Temples is the main focus on this day, we also commemorate several other tragic events in Jewish history. On the 9th day of Av in 135 CE the Romans defeated Simeon bar Kochba, who led the Jewish rebellion against them. We also recall that the Jews of York, England were killed in the year 1190; Jews were expelled from England in 1290 and from Spain in 1492; the Nazis deported Jews from the Warsaw Ghetto to the Treblinka concentration camp in 1942. While there is debate as to whether any or all of these events actually occurred on the 9th of Av, these great losses are mourned on Tisha B'Av.

During the weeks leading up to Tisha B'Av the season of mourning begins. On the 1st of Av the restrictions intensify. Traditionally, there are no marriages during the three weeks prior to Tisha B'Av; people do not get haircuts or new clothing; meat is not eaten; artwork is not created; pleasurable activities are avoided. The day of Tisha B'Av itself is a day of fasting, from sundown to sundown. Because it is a day of mourning, strict observers do not engage in any joyful or pleasurable activities. On years that Tisha B'Av falls on Shabbat, the fast is postponed until Sunday. Interestingly, the day of mourning actually ends with an air of hope, as legend has it that the Messiah will be born on Tisha B'Av.

In more recent years Tisha B'Av has been undergoing new interpretations. Some use this time to mourn the victims of the Holocaust, the dropping of atomic bombs on Hiroshima and Nagasaki, and other instances of overwhelming violence against groups of people. Tisha B'Av lends itself to taking action on behalf of political refugees, victims of war, and those who are targeted by ethnic violence, as we can readily see that their story and ours bear some resemblance to each other. Consider ways of making a difference by learning their stories and through *tzedaka* (charitable giving) and *gemilut hasadim* (acts of kindness) – the two branches of *tikkun olam* (repairing the world).

In addition to remembering some of the tragedies that have befallen the Jewish people throughout history, we might also wish to acknowledge the strength and perseverance demonstrated in order for Judaism to have survived all of these ordeals. For Jews and others to endure such attacks is a testimony to the courage and resilience of the human spirit.

11. Rosh Ha-Shanah

Falling on the 1st day of the month of Tishri (during September or October on the civil calendar) is the Jewish new year, Rosh Ha-Shanah ("Head of the Year"). This manifestation of the holiday seems to have gained popularity during the Talmudic period, which dates from 70 CE to 500 CE. Prior to that there was an autumn festival, which is mentioned in the Torah – though details about its nature are not provided. Rosh Ha-Shanah is most likely based in part on religious observances that predate Judaism, as ancient cultures in Babylonia and the surrounding areas commonly held coronation festivals in the fall. One legacy of this is the strong image of God as king in the Rosh Ha-Shanah liturgy. Rosh Ha-Shanah is celebrated for two days, both in Israel and the Diaspora.

The Jewish calendar marks time from the creation of the world, believed at the time the calendar was developed to be 3761 BCE. On Rosh Ha-Shanah the calendar advances another year. In celebration, sweet foods are enjoyed to symbolize a wish for a sweet new year. This includes eating *challah* and apples dipped in honey, *kugel* (noodle pudding), honey cakes, *tzimmes* (a mixture of carrots, yams, and honey), and *teiglach* (small balls or knots of dough that are boiled or baked in honey syrup). For vegans and others who do not consume honey, a substitution of maple syrup or agave nectar can be easily made.

On Rosh Ha-Shanah the *challah* is made in the shape of a round loaf instead of the typical oblong braided loaf baked throughout the rest of the year. The round shape symbolizes the unending circle of life, the cyclical nature of the year, or the crown of God. Some people have a tradition of continuing to bake *challah* in a round shape and dipping it in honey until the end of Simchat Torah, which falls about three weeks later.

The *challah* for Rosh Ha-Shanah is sometimes baked in the shape of a ladder or a bird, symbolizing the wish for our prayers to rise all the way to heaven. The ladder shape may also indicate that we will either ascend or descend the ladder of life, depending on how we are judged by God. The *challah* may be made with raisins to make it particularly sweet.

There is a custom of trying new or unusual fruits for Rosh Ha-Shanah, particularly on the second night. (A pomegranate is a popular choice for this custom, with its multitude of seeds symbolizing the 613 Commandments given to us by God.) Some people cut carrots into rounds that look like coins, representing wishes for a good income during the new year.

Rosh Ha-Shanah is strongly connected to Yom Kippur, which falls ten days later, and the two are often called the High Holy Days or High Holidays. The period between Rosh Ha-Shanah and Yom Kippur is referred to as *Yamim Noraim* ("Days of Awe") or *Aseret Yemei Teshuvah* ("Ten Days of Repentance") and is the most serious, somber time of the Jewish holiday cycle. This is when we reflect upon our actions of the past year, ask forgiveness for our offenses against other people and against God, forgive those who have offended us (if we are capable of sincerely doing so), and commit to living a more just and honorable life during the coming year. The goal is not to be perfect but to be the best individuals we are capable of being. During the Days of Awe, many Jewish people give *tzedaka* (charitable donations) to organizations that work to alleviate hunger. Personal action may also be taken to assist those who are hungry.

As we recognize the wrongs we have committed during the past year, we should feel remorseful and seek to repair the harm where possible, apologizing to and asking forgiveness from people we have hurt. While we can ask God to forgive us for sins committed against Him, He cannot forgive us for wrongs we have inflicted upon other people. Only those whom we have offended can forgive us for those deeds, and we are therefore responsible for reconciling our own relationships. The process of self-reflection and atonement can be difficult at times. But it is not something to be feared or avoided, since the goal is to promote positive inner changes and improve our relationships with others. (If we apologize to a person three times, we are considered to be forgiven even if the person chooses not to accept our apologies.)

Rosh Ha-Shanah is sometimes called *Yom Ha-Din* ("The Day of Judgment"), and there is strong imagery of God as judge and king during this time of year. It is said that each person passes before God on Rosh Ha-Shanah, and He judges each of us – inscribing our name in the Book of Life if we are righteous or in the Book of Death if we are wicked. The vast majority of people fall somewhere in between these two extremes and have until Yom Kippur to repent, for on Yom Kippur our fate is sealed as we are written in either the Book of Life or the Book of Death. The words "life" and "death" refer not to our physical bodies but to our spiritual selves. The traditional belief is that God punishes the wicked and rewards the good, so there is great incentive to atone for our sins and wrongdoings before Yom Kippur.

Rosh Ha-Shanah is a time of great hope. It is an opportunity to focus on our human potential for positive change and self-improvement. We have the ability to become better human beings and recommit ourselves to living in accordance with our personal values. This is a good time to ask ourselves what we want out of life, think about what guides our behaviors, evaluate whether our behaviors are getting us closer to or further from our goals in life, choose which obligations we want to commit to fulfilling in the coming year, and heal our relationships with others. Rosh Ha-Shanah separates what was from what will be, the past from the future – both in terms of the calendar and our individual journeys as human beings.

Looking within ourselves, evaluating our behaviors of the past year, and making plans to better ourselves during the coming year is a huge task. Because such introspection requires significant time, the process begins during the month of Elul, the month preceding Rosh Ha-Shanah.

The *shofar*, an ancient instrument made from a ram's horn, is sounded every day of Elul and on Rosh Ha-Shanah, except on the Sabbath. (If the first day of Rosh Ha-Shanah falls on the Sabbath, then the *shofar* is sounded the following day.) The blast of the *shofar* can be interpreted in several different ways. It has been described as being able to frighten off evil spirits, preventing them from leading people astray. Some say the blast of the *shofar* awakens our minds and souls so that we become aware of how we are living our lives. It can also be considered a call to battle against our inner demons.

The *shofar* is sounded in a particular pattern of long, short, and staccato blasts. The sound it makes is mysterious, haunting, primitive, and soul-stirring. The sound of the *shofar* triggers both excitement and fear within us, a good reflection of the way many of us feel about change and the uncertainty that accompanies the approaching Day of Judgment. The *shofar* is sounded during synagogue services, and some people sound their own *shofar* at home.

During the weeks leading up to Rosh Ha-Shanah, many people visit the graves of deceased family members and others who are particularly important to them. This is a meaningful way of remembering the past while looking forward to the new year. If you know someone who has lost a family member during the past year, you may want to visit with them and remember their loved one with them at this time. Comforting those who are in mourning is a *mitzvah* – a commandment from God – and an act of kindness. As Rosh Ha-Shanah approaches, cards are sent to family and friends to wish them a good and sweet new year.

There is a traditional activity called *tashlich* ("cast" or "send"), which is performed on the afternoon of the first day of Rosh Ha-Shanah. (If the first day of Rosh Ha-Shanah falls on Shabbat, then *tashlich* is done on the second day.) *Tashlich* is performed by tossing bread crumbs into a flowing body of water, symbolically casting away our sins.

At home, we might invite guests to share a Rosh Ha-Shanah dinner, which includes some of the special foods mentioned earlier in this chapter. Festival candles are customarily lit. Traditional blessings for this dinner include *kiddush* for the wine, *ha-motzi* for the bread, the blessing for fruit (recited before eating the apples), and – on the second night –

the *shehecheyanu* blessing of gratitude.

On Rosh Ha-Shanah the calendar advances by another year, marking time on earth and in the wider universe. As we recognize this absolute passage of time, we also note our relative progress on our human journeys. We reflect upon our actions of the past year and prepare to make improvements for the coming year. The message of Rosh Ha-Shanah is that a person can improve their fate through repentance and righteous actions. This is not an easy process, but positive change is an achievable goal.

Rosh Ha-Shanah: Blessings and Candle Lighting Information

Lighting the festival candles

On Rosh Ha-Shanah, festival candles are lit on both evenings of the holiday. Some people light two candles, while others prefer to light one candle for each member of the family. (Please read Important Information about Candles on page 32.) Remember that the Jewish calendar marks days from sunset to sunset, meaning that on the civil calendar the holidays begin on the previous evening.

Blessing for lighting the festival candles

Baruch Atah, Adonai Eloheinu, Melech ha-olam,
asher kid'shanu b'mitzvotav v'tzivanu l'hadlik ner shel yom tov.

Blessed are You, Lord our God, King of the universe,
who has sanctified us with His commandments
and has commanded us to kindle the light of the festival day.

Blessing for lighting the festival candles on Shabbat

When the candles are lit on a Friday evening,
the blessing is slightly different.

Baruch Atah, Adonai Eloheinu, Melech ha-olam, asher kid'shanu
b'mitzvotav v'tzivanu l'hadlik ner shel Shabot v'shel yom tov.

Blessed are You, Lord our God, King of the universe,
who has sanctified us with His commandments
and has commanded us to kindle the light
of the Sabbath and the festival day.

55

Kiddush: the blessing for wine (or grape juice)

Baruch Atah, Adonai Eloheinu, Melech ha-olam, borei p'ri hagafen.

Blessed are You, Lord Our God, King of the universe,
creator of the fruit of the vine.

Ha-Motzi: the blessing for bread

Baruch Atah, Adonai Eloheinu, Melech ha-olam,
ha-motzi lehem min ha-aretz.

Blessed are You, Lord our God, King of the universe,
who brings forth bread from the earth.

Ha-Etz: the blessing for fruits grown on trees

Baruch Atah, Adonai Eloheinu, Melech ha-olam, borei p'ri ha-etz.

Blessed are You, Lord our God, King of the universe,
creator of the fruit of the tree.

After dipping the apple in honey and eating it, recite the following:
Y'hi ratzon mil'fanekha, Adonai Eloheinu vei'lohei avoteinu,
h't'chadeish aleinu shanah tovah um'tukah.

May it be Your will, Lord our God and God of our ancestors,
that You renew for us a good and sweet year.

Shehecheyanu: the blessing of gratitude

The *shehechyanu* is recited on the second night of Rosh Ha-Shanah
prior to eating a new fruit or a fruit that you have not had for some time.

Baruch Atah, Adonai Eloheinu, Melech ha-olam,
shehecheyanu v'kiyimanu v'higi'anu lazman hazeh.

Blessed are You, Lord our God, King of the universe,
who has granted us life, sustained us, and enabled us to reach this season.

12. Yom Kippur

Yom Kippur, "The Day of Atonement," is the holiest, most solemn day on the Jewish calendar. It is observed on the 10th day of the month of Tishri. During the Days of Awe, the time between Rosh Ha-Shanah and Yom Kippur, we engage in self-reflection, atone for our wrongdoings, and heal our damaged relationships with others. Yom Kippur is the last day to make amends, for it is on this day that God is said to pass final judgment on us for the year. On this day God inscribes each of us into the Book of Life if we are deemed to be righteous or the Book of Death if we are judged to be wicked.

Yom Kippur was not always a solemn occasion. It appears that in ancient times it was a more joyful celebration; over time, it evolved to become the somber holiday we recognize today. With the destruction of the Second Temple in 70 CE, animal sacrifices on Yom Kippur came to be replaced by prayer. Several hundred years later, the Talmud instructed Jews that they were to fast during Yom Kippur, from sunset to sunset. People were also not to bathe, anoint the body with oil, wear leather shoes, have sexual relations, or engage in several other specific physical activities on Yom Kippur. These restrictions are still observed by many Jewish people today.

On Yom Kippur we hold up a mirror to ourselves to see who we really are, and we consider who we want to be. We confront our shortcomings and identify our true selves. We stand before God, the judge, who knows all and sees all. As the final Day of Judgment, Yom Kippur is traditionally a day spent immersed in prayer and meditation at the synagogue. People often wear white – the color of purity and also the color of the burial shroud, reminding us of our own mortality and connecting us to those who have come and gone before us. Yom Kippur services conclude at the end of the day with a final sounding of the *shofar*.

The most important ritual of Yom Kippur is engaging in self-reflection, with the ultimate goal of putting thoughts into action in order to achieve self-improvement. Being sorry for transgressions is not sufficient; we must take action to make our lives and relationships better. As humans, we have a responsibility to help heal the world. It is not God's role to fix the problems we have created; we must resolve these difficult situations on our own.

During meditations on Yom Kippur, some people reflect upon the Jewish people's Covenant with God. If you will recall, the celebration of Shavuot is primarily a commemoration of the Israelites receiving the law of God at Mount Sinai. The Ten Commandments indicate that we are to live with high standards of behavior and treat each other with respect. Now, at Yom Kippur, there is another opportunity to evaluate whether or not we are living up to these standards and make improvements where necessary.

On the evening of the arrival of Yom Kippur, we light festival candles, as well as a *yizkor* memorial candle to remember loved ones who have died. The evening meal, eaten prior to sundown and the candle lighting, should be substantial but fairly bland so that it doesn't trigger thirst as we begin our 24-hour fast.

The purpose of fasting on Yom Kippur is to help us focus on our meditations. Without the distraction of food and other physical comforts, we are able to increase our spiritual awareness and delve deeper into our thoughts and self-reflection. We do not fast to punish ourselves but to set ourselves free. As our bodies are purged by the fast from food, our souls are renewed and our spiritual slates are cleaned. In abstaining from pleasurable physical activities, we encourage ourselves to engage in positive spiritual endeavors. Some consider the 24-hour fast to be a small taste of death in order to more fully appreciate life.

Those who choose to fast do not eat or drink anything from sundown on the evening that begins Yom Kippur until the sun sets at the end of the 10th day of Tishri. Those who are ill, in fragile health, have serious medical conditions, or are pregnant or breastfeeding are exempt from fasting. Children who are under 13 years of age are also exempt, though starting at about age nine, children might skip breakfast or have lighter meals than normal during the day, if they choose to do so.

Fasting serves as a reminder that we are more than just our physical selves. We feel the pangs of hunger but are able to confront and move beyond our physical urges through meditation, prayer, and focusing on the spirit. As the body and soul work together, we see that fasting can help us on our quest to reach our spiritual selves. Fasting can also teach us about hunger, encouraging us to help those who are persistently hungry because they cannot afford to buy enough food.

Following sundown on Yom Kippur, we break the fast, usually with family and friends. This should be a light meal that isn't too spicy, so as not to put stress on empty stomachs. While there isn't a standard menu for this occasion, it should be a simple meal requiring little preparation. After all, we should be focused on our meditations during Yom Kippur, not working in the kitchen to make a fancy dinner. (Also, it is very difficult to prepare a meal while abstaining from food.) Bagels with toppings such as lox, hummus, cream cheese, or other spreads is a popular meal to break the fast. Vegetables with dip, light sandwiches or wraps, salads, or even ordering out for pizza are just a few ideas for simple meals. Alternatively, meals can be prepared prior to the fast. A *kugel* or casserole can be preassembled so that it just needs to be put in the oven toward the end of the fast; or it can be baked ahead of time and then quickly reheated.

With the close of Yom Kippur comes a dramatic change in mood. The solemnity of Yom Kippur quickly gives way to sheer delight as we break the fast and set our sights ahead to the most joyous festival of the Jewish calendar, Sukkot, which begins in only four days.

Yom Kippur: Blessings and Candle Lighting Information

Lighting the festival candles

Festival candles are traditionally lit to usher in Yom Kippur, the holiest day on the Jewish calendar. Some people light two candles, while others prefer to light one candle for each member of the family. (Please read Important Information about Candles on page 32.) Remember that the Jewish calendar marks days from sunset to sunset, meaning that on the civil calendar the holidays begin on the previous evening.

Blessing for lighting the festival candles

Baruch Atah, Adonai Eloheinu, Melech ha-olam,
asher kid'shanu b'mitzvotav v'tzivanu l'hadlik ner shel yom tov.

Blessed are You, Lord our God, King of the universe,
who has sanctified us with His commandments
and has commanded us to kindle the light of the festival day.

Blessing for lighting the festival candles on Shabbat

When the candles are lit on a Friday evening,
the blessing is slightly different.

Baruch Atah, Adonai Eloheinu, Melech ha-olam, asher kid'shanu
b'mitzvotav v'tzivanu l'hadlik ner shel Shabot v'shel yom tov.

Blessed are You, Lord our God, King of the universe,
who has sanctified us with His commandments
and has commanded us to kindle the light
of the Sabbath and the festival day.

Yizkor memorial candle

This candle, referred to as *yahrzeit* in Yiddish, is lit in honor of loved ones who have passed away. It may be lit on Yom Kippur. It is a good opportunity to think about your departed loved ones, and you may want to say a few words about them or recite a relevant poem or prayer. The *yizkor* ("remember") has enough wax to burn for a minimum of 24 hours and is traditionally lit on certain Jewish holidays as well as on the anniversary of the loved one's death. *Yizkor* memorial candles are lit as a cultural custom rather than as a traditional religious obligation, so they may take any form and be lit in whatever manner is meaningful to you.

When breaking the fast at sundown at the end of Yom Kippur, you may recite these blessings:

Kiddush: the blessing for wine (or grape juice)
Baruch Atah, Adonai Eloheinu, Melech ha-olam, borei p'ri hagafen.

Blessed are You, Lord Our God, King of the universe, creator of the fruit of the vine.

Ha-Motzi: the blessing for bread
Baruch Atah, Adonai Eloheinu, Melech ha-olam, ha-motzi lehem min ha-aretz.

Blessed are You, Lord our God, King of the universe who brings forth bread from the earth.

13. Sukkot

The autumn festival of Sukkot is an incredibly joyful time on the Jewish calendar. It begins on the 15th day of Tishri – right on the heels of Yom Kippur, the most somber of the Jewish holidays. Sukkot lasts for seven days, though it is functionally extended by another day or two with the observance of two other holidays, Shemini Atzeret and Simchat Torah. (These two holidays are discussed in more detail in the following chapter.) Sukkot is sometimes referred to simply as *Ha-Hag*, "The Holiday," and is thought to have been the most important Jewish festival in Biblical times.

As with the other two pilgrimage festivals, Pesach and Shavuot, Sukkot began as an agricultural observance. It marked the time of the fall harvest in the land of Israel, the final harvest before winter. The last of the fruits are gathered, including grapes and olives – of special significance as ingredients to make wine and oil. The agricultural origin of this festival gives Sukkot one of its other names, *Hag Ha-Asif* – "Festival of Ingathering" or "Harvest Festival."

In ancient times pilgrims would journey to Jerusalem for the autumn harvest festival to make offerings and perform animal sacrifices at the the First Temple – the Temple of Solomon. Following the Temple's destruction at the hands of the Babylonians in the year 586 BCE, Jewish festivals could not be observed at the traditional holy place. But with the fall of the Babylonian empire some 50 years later, the Jewish people were able to celebrate in Jerusalem once again. It was at this point that the nature of Sukkot began to shift from an agricultural festival to a particularly joyful commemoration of the Israelites' 40-year journey through the desert in search of the Promised Land. In this way, the three pilgrimage festivals are linked both agriculturally and Biblically. Through these three festivals, we commemorate the annual harvest cycles as well as the stories of the Exodus from Egypt, the giving of the Ten Commandments at Mount Sinai, and the 40 years of travel through the desert. Taken together, they combine to create an extended story of the ancient Israelites' journey from slavery to their establishment of a Jewish nation.

During the High Holy Days of Rosh Ha-Shanah and Yom Kippur, the image of God is as a judge and king, a father figure who rules with a firm hand. Now, at Sukkot, the imagery surrounding God changes to one of a mother figure, a nurturing and protective entity. God's loving, caring aspects are celebrated, for both providing a good harvest and protecting the wandering Israelites as they made their way through the inhospitable desert. According to legend, God traveled with the Israelites, housed in a portable temple, or tabernacle. He protected the Israelites, provided for their survival, and gave them direction in the wilderness where there were few resources.

Traveling through the desert for 40 years, the Israelites built *sukkot*, portable shelters constructed of dry palm leaves and branches. To remind ourselves of their journey and of God sheltering them against danger, we build our own *sukkah* ("booth" or "hut") in which to celebrate the holiday of Sukkot. Erected in homage to nomadic life, these structures must be temporary, coming down after the end of Sukkot.

The building of the holiday *sukkah* is a joyful event and can be started as early as sundown at the end of Yom Kippur, though the *sukkah* is not used until the beginning of Sukkot. The *sukkah* must have at least three sides. If possible, it should be built under the open sky and not beneath the overhang of a house, other structure, or heavy foliage. It may be constructed to stand apart from the house, on the deck or balcony of the house, or against the house – using the house as one of the *sukkah*'s walls.

The most stringent regulations about the construction of the *sukkah* involve the roof, or *sechach* ("covering"). The roof must be made of organic materials that have grown in the ground and been removed, such as branches from trees. It should be loosely thatched, providing a certain amount of shade but still allowing a person to view stars at night when looking up from inside the *sukkah*. Because Sukkot falls in the middle of the month, it begins on or near the full moon, which might also be seen through the roof of the *sukkah*. The walls of the *sukkah* should be strong enough to withstand normal winds but not necessarily a powerful gale. The structure should help to protect us from sun, rain, and wind while still leaving us open to the elements and to the world.

Creativity is encouraged in the construction of the *sukkah*, which should be decorated and have beauty. The following are popular decorations for the *sukkah*: artwork or paper chains; products from the harvest, such as gourds, wreaths, or corn stalks; debris from your property, such as branches, vines, or leftover growth from the garden; seasonal fruits and vegetables; and flowers. But do not feel that you have to limit yourself to these basic suggestions, since the *sukkah* should reflect your own creativity and personality.

There is an enormous variety of *sukkah* designs and materials. The *sukkah* might feature wooden, bamboo, or PVC poles; gardening lattice; painted bed sheets; ropes; or any number of other materials. Many people furnish their *sukkah* with lawn chairs and tables. An online search will yield numerous ideas for you to construct your own *sukkah*.

The Torah instructs us to actually live in the *sukkah* for the week of Sukkot, and it is considered particularly important to enjoy dinner there on the first evening of the holiday. Many people eat at least some of their meals in the *sukkah*, and some choose to spend a night or more there as well. It is good to be able to relax, read, and socialize in the *sukkah*, and time spent there should feel pleasurable.

While living in the *sukkah* is one of the commandments of Sukkot, we are also required by the Torah to be blissful and rejoice during the holiday. Therefore, if staying in the *sukkah* makes us feel too uncomfortable – to the point of not being able to enjoy the experience – then we are instructed by religious authorities to leave the *sukkah*. Being unhappy during Sukkot is considered far worse than leaving the *sukkah*. Indeed, if there are uncomfortable weather conditions, such as rain, a thunderstorm, or snow, we are specifically ordered by many rabbis to leave the *sukkah* for the comfort of our permanent home. It is not deemed noble to suffer during the joyful Sukkot celebration.

One of the themes of Sukkot is hospitality. We should share our shelters, impermanent though they are, with others. Invite family and friends – Jews and non-Jews – to join you in your *sukkah*. This should be a time of merrymaking, so feel free to sing, play musical instruments, tell stories, or entertain yourselves in other ways.

Long ago, families made it a point to invite the poor to dine and stay in their *sukkah*. Today you might make a charitable donation or give your time or resources to an agency that helps the homeless or those transitioning out of homelessness in your area. You may consider helping someone with a household repair project. Or, in honor of the Israelites' search for a homeland, you might choose to support an organization that serves immigrants or refugees, particularly those fleeing from oppression, with your time or charitable donation. Certainly, assisting the hungry would also be appropriate, since Sukkot celebrates the fall harvest. Think about inviting those with more hidden needs to your *sukkah*. It would be an act of kindness to share your *sukkah* with guests whose spirits are in need of joy, or with individuals who may be lonely and in need of company.

On Sukkot we invite not only real guests, but symbolic guests – *ushpizin* – as well, one on each of the festival's seven days. Traditionally, the *ushpizin* are Jewish patriarchs: Abraham, Isaac, Jacob, Joseph, David, Moses, and Aaron. All of these figures were wanderers or travelers, making it especially fitting that they should be offered shelter in the *sukkah* to come and rest. These specific guests are honored for their dedication to God and for their contributions to the world. They embody characteristics that we might strive to incorporate in ourselves. Abraham, Isaac, and Jacob exhibited qualities of hospitality, sacrifice, humbleness, passion, and faithfulness. Moses and Aaron had great devotion to God, while Joseph personified holiness and spiritual foundation. David demonstrated courage in his decision to rule by the principles of the Torah. Inviting ancestral guests reminds us of our history and heritage.

In more recent times, some families have chosen to invite Jewish matriarchs and heroines to the *sukkah* as well. These might include figures such as Sarah, Rebecca, Rachel, Leah, Miriam, Abigail, and Esther. Families may also invite famous Jewish men and women from throughout history, such as Judah Maccabee, Maimonides, Albert Einstein, Golda Meir, and Hanna Szenesh. Indeed, guests from any heritage who have played important roles in social justice, such as Martin Luther King, Jr. or Susan B. Anthony, may be considered appropriate to invite to your *sukkah*.

Whoever the symbolic guests are, the purpose is to inspire us to become better people ourselves, through their hope, courage, faithfulness, and actions. A chair may be set aside in the *sukkah* for that day's guest to be seated. You may think about or discuss with your family and friends the characteristics and achievements of your guests. Who are they? What did they do? Why are they important? You may also imagine having conversations with the symbolic guests. What might they say about events that took place during their time? What might they think about today's world?

Another tradition of Sukkot is the gathering of the four species, or *arba minim*. As a commemoration of the agricultural origin of Sukkot, we gather (or symbolically harvest) the following: an *etrog* (a citron, rather similar to a large, bumpy lemon, that perhaps was the fruit from the Tree of Knowledge described in the Bible), a *lulav* (branch from a palm tree), three *hadasim* (branches from a myrtle bush), and two *aravot* (branches from a willow tree). The three species of tree branches are tied together, while the *etrog* is kept in a special *etrog* container. On each day of Sukkot, except on the Sabbath, there is a special ritual of shaking or waving the four species. (This is detailed at the end of this chapter.) Following Sukkot, some people make fruit preserves out of the *etrog* in order to enjoy it several months later on the holiday of Tu B'Shevat. If you are interested in purchasing the *arba minim* for Sukkot, they are most easily acquired through a synagogue or a store specializing in Judaica. It is considered important to find the most beautiful, perfect members of the four species available.

The four species are said to represent four different kinds of Jews. The *etrog* has both taste and fragrance, symbolizing those who both have knowledge and engage in good deeds. The *lulav* produces dates, having taste but no fragrance, symbolizing knowledge only. The *hadas* has fragrance but no taste, symbolizing good deeds only. The *aravah* has neither taste nor fragrance, symbolizing a lack of both knowledge and good deeds. Just as the branches and the *etrog* are held together during the waving of the four species, so are all Jews bound together by our history, heritage, and culture. We complement each other and compensate for one another. This metaphor may be extended to mean all people, not only Jews. The symbols of knowledge and good deeds could also be used to illustrate how we as individuals might act under different circumstances.

Another interpretation of the four species is that each species represents a different part of the human body and experience, reminding us to serve God and/or humanity with our entire selves. The *etrog* is said to symbolize the heart and understanding; the palm branch depicts the spine and strength; myrtle signifies the eyes and enlightenment; and willow represents the lips and prayer.

On the first night of Sukkot, there are several traditional blessings to usher in the festival. First, the festival candles are lit. Then there is the *kiddush* over the wine, the blessing for the *sukkah* (if you are celebrating in a *sukkah*), the *shehecheyanu* blessing of gratitude, the waving of the four species (if you have them), and *ha-motzi* over the bread. During the rest of the festival of Sukkot, blessings for the *sukkah*, wine, and bread may be repeated as necessary, and the *arba minim* may be waved once each day, though not on the Sabbath. (See the end of this chapter for more information about the blessings for Sukkot.)

Sukkot shares some interesting parallels with Pesach. Both holidays present us with an opportunity to examine our assumptions about our basic needs. During Pesach we consider our feelings about food, specifically as they relate to *hametz*. We think about what it means to us to observe the special dietary restrictions of Pesach and confront our own fears and discomforts about changing our habits with food. As described in the chapter about Pesach, in restricting our choices, we may set ourselves free.

During Sukkot, another extended holiday, we reevaluate our relationship with shelter. We experience joy and excitement in constructing the *sukkah*; but we may also feel discomfort or fear in spending considerable amounts of time in the small and rather flimsy structure, which lacks the comforts and possessions of our homes. The *sukkah* leaves us exposed to the elements, helping us to imagine the experience of the wandering Israelites, as well as of homeless people today.

But focusing only on the weakness of the *sukkah*'s structure would severely limit our understanding of the *sukkah* and ourselves. While the *sukkah* is a temporary and somewhat ineffective shelter, it does provide us with an experience not afforded to us by our permanent homes. Our permanent homes protect us from the elements and give us the comfort of many material possessions – but they also separate us from our neighbors and nature and can be seen as prisons in which we are trapped. Being outdoors and spending time in the *sukkah* with family, friends, and neighbors allows us to reconnect with nature and with one another in joyful celebration.

During Sukkot we might glimpse and even come to understand that the comforts and possessions of our homes can be another form of slavery or idolatry – if we value them above our relationships with people, nature, and God. True security is not gained through the accumulation of material possessions, and those very comforts may well trap us in the end. The joy of Sukkot may be most deeply felt by spending time in a temporary shelter that is free of too many possessions and is open to nonmaterial gifts.

The *sukkah* serves as a spiritual shelter much more than as a physical shelter. By leaving the security of our permanent homes, we are able to experience an amazing sense of freedom. Just as freeing ourselves from *hametz* during Pesach enables us to break our slavery to food, leaving our homes during Sukkot helps us to break our slavery to possessions. It is a paradox in which we attain freedom by restricting our choices. This has some similarities to the story of Shavuot, in which the

Israelites experienced freedom by choosing to devote themselves to serving and obeying God.

When the ancient Israelites left Egypt, they were afraid of what the future held for them. Many preferred the harsh life of slavery to the uncertainties of freedom. They brought *matzah* (the bread of poverty) and temporary shelters called *sukkot* on their journey, and somehow they had enough to survive. God's sheltering presence protected them and sustained them as they traveled from slavery to freedom. They found security within their insecurity, having both nothing and everything.

Sukkot is referred to as *Zeman Simchateinu*, "The Season of Our Rejoicing." We express our joy and gratitude for the harvest, for having so recently completed the process of repentance on Yom Kippur, and for having everything we need in our temporary *sukkah*.

Sukkot: Blessings and Candle Lighting Information

Lighting the festival candles

On the first night of Sukkot, festival candles are lit. Some people light two candles, while others prefer to light one candle for each member of the family. (Please read Important Information about Candles on page 32.) Remember that the Jewish calendar marks days from sunset to sunset, meaning that on the civil calendar the holidays begin on the previous evening.

Blessing for lighting the festival candles

Baruch Atah, Adonai Eloheinu, Melech ha-olam,
asher kid'shanu b'mitzvotav v'tzivanu l'hadlik ner shel yom tov.

Blessed are You, Lord our God, King of the universe,
who has sanctified us with His commandments
and has commanded us to kindle the light of the festival day.

Blessing for lighting the festival candles on Shabbat
When the candles are lit on a Friday evening,
the blessing is slightly different.

Baruch Atah, Adonai Eloheinu, Melech ha-olam, asher kid'shanu
b'mitzvotav v'tzivanu l'hadlik ner shel Shabot v'shel yom tov.

Blessed are You, Lord our God, King of the universe,
who has sanctified us with His commandments
and has commanded us to kindle the light
of the Sabbath and the festival day.

Kiddush: the blessing for wine (or grape juice)

This can be recited whenever you have wine or grape juice. Performing this ritual on the first night of Sukkot is considered to be particularly important.

Baruch Atah, Adonai Eloheinu, Melech ha-olam, borei p'ri hagafen.

Blessed are You, Lord Our God, King of the universe,
creator of the fruit of the vine.

The blessing for the sukkah

Recite this during Sukkot whenever you are celebrating in a *sukkah*.

*Baruch Atah, Adonai Eloheinu, Melech ha-olam,
asher kid'shanu b'mitzvotav v'tzivanu leisheiv basukah.*

Blessed are You, Lord our God, King of the universe,
who has sanctified us with His commandments
and has commanded us to dwell in the sukkah.

Shehecheyanu: the blessing of gratitude

The *shehecheyanu* is recited only on the first night of Sukkot.

*Baruch Atah, Adonai Eloheinu, Melech ha-olam,
shehecheyanu v'kiyimanu v'higi'anu lazman hazeh.*

Blessed are You, Lord our God, King of the universe,
who has granted us life, sustained us, and enabled us to reach this season.

The shaking or waving of the lulav

This ritual is performed every day of Sukkot, except on the Sabbath. The bound branches are held in the right hand with the spine facing the person holding it. The *etrog* is held in the left hand with the *pittam* (bump on the pointed end, on the side opposite of where the fruit was once attached to the tree) facing down. While holding the *lulav* and *etrog* so that they are touching each other, recite the blessing of the four species:

Baruch Atah, Adonai Eloheinu, Melech ha-olam,
asher kid'shanu b'mitzvotav, v'tzivanu al netilat lulav.

Blessed are You, Lord our God, King of the universe,
who has sanctified us with His commandments
and commanded us concerning the shaking of the *lulav*.

Now turn the *etrog* so the *pittam* faces upward. Shake the four species together in six directions: east, west, north, south, above, and below. Give three shakes in each direction.

Ha-Motzi: the blessing for bread

This should be recited whenever you have *challah* in the *sukkah* or eat a meal that includes bread.

Baruch Atah, Adonai Eloheinu, Melech ha-olam
ha-motzi lehem min ha-aretz.

Blessed are You, Lord our God, King of the universe,
who brings forth bread from the earth.

14. Shemini Atzeret and Simchat Torah

Following the final day of Sukkot are the celebrations of Shemini Atzeret and Simchat Torah. Some consider these to be extensions of Sukkot, while others observe them as independent holidays. Shemini Atzeret and Simchat Torah are both celebrated on the 22nd day of Tishri (the day after the end of Sukkot) in Israel and by Reform and Reconstructionist congregations in the Diaspora. Most Conservative and Orthodox communities in the Diaspora observe Shemini Atzeret for two days, focusing on Simchat Torah on the second day (the 23rd day of Tishri). After these two holidays are over, it is time to dismantle the *sukkah*.

Shemini Atzeret was more widely celebrated many years ago, when people were more closely connected to the land and the harvest. A special prayer for rain is the main focus of Shemini Atzeret. The prayer for rain, or *geshem*, was extremely important to the ancient Jews and is still significant today, since a good amount of precipitation during the rainy season sets the stage for a successful future harvest. Indeed, if rain does not fall in the land of Israel within several weeks of Sukkot, the next season's crops may be in danger of failing. The *geshem* may be translated as follows:

For you are Hashem our God
Who makes the wind blow and the rain descend.

For blessing and not for curse.

For life and not for death.

For plenty and not for scarcity.

The language used indicates a desire for rainfall to promote fertile land that will benefit the people. Rain is recognized as a source of life, a necessity for a successful harvest. But the text could also be considered a prayer for balance, that the rainfall shouldn't be too extreme or violent, lest it create hardship.

On this day you may want to consider the relationship between weather and agriculture. Think about the sometimes delicate balance between insufficient rainfall and excessive rainfall, as well as the impact of other climate conditions on food production. Remember that in late autumn and in winter the earth is preparing for the following spring, and that our future crops will reflect the weather conditions of today.

Although we do not recite the blessing for the *sukkah* or wave the four species as we did during Sukkot, we may still have meals in the *sukkah* during Shemini Atzeret. Festival candles are lit, a *yizkor* memorial candle for the deceased is also lit, and the *shehecheyanu* blessing of gratitude is recited.

Simchat Torah translates as "Joy of the Torah" or "Rejoicing in the Law" and is a jubilant celebration of the annual cycle of Torah readings. It is on this day that the last Torah portion (the end of Deuteronomy) is read, followed by the first portion (the story of creation in Genesis). Coming to the end of the Torah and immediately starting at the beginning once again infuses Simchat Torah with strong imagery of the never-ending cycle of learning the Torah.

During the course of a year, the entire Torah is read during synagogue services, though there are several variations as to how this is accomplished. In Israel and in Orthodox communities in the Diaspora, all of the Torah portions are read during services, a custom that developed in Babylonia in the seventh century CE. The vast majority of Conservative and Reform synagogues in the United States also read the Torah on a one-year cycle, though only about one-third of each portion is read. Some congregations read the Torah on a three-year cycle.

Regardless of how the Torah is read, all congregations celebrate Simchat Torah by singing and dancing with the Torah scrolls around the synagogue as part of a special service.

The cause for celebration on Simchat Torah isn't simply the recitation of the Torah year after year, for the Torah is not considered a document to be mindlessly read. The joy comes in being intellectually and spiritually nurtured by "the Tree of Life" that is the Torah. Although it is the same text that is read every year, each time it is read we have the capacity and potential to gain greater knowledge and understanding of the Torah. Through studying and appreciating the Torah, we hope to become better people. As one prayer for Simchat Torah expresses:

> Source of Life,
> every year You plant within us a new tree of life.
> May it be Your will that this year
> our interpretations will blossom forth
> kindness and not cruelty,
> wisdom and not foolishness,
> awareness and not thoughtlessness.
> May You teach us a Torah of love
> that will nourish us in the coming days at every hour.

Simchat Torah may be observed by reading the final portion of Deuteronomy followed by the first portion of Genesis. As with Shavuot, the other holiday that focuses on the Torah, this is a good opportunity to consider what the Torah means to you. Think about what commitment, if any, you want to make to studying the Torah.

Shemini Atzeret and Simchat Torah: Blessings and Candle Lighting Information

Although we may continue to enjoy time in the *sukkah*, we do not recite the blessings for the *sukkah* or wave the four species on Shemini Atzeret and Simchat Torah. But the *kiddush* for the wine and *ha-motzi* for the bread may still be recited as necessary. In observance of Shemini Atzeret, festival candles and a *yizkor* memorial candle may be lit.

Lighting the festival candles

Festival candles may be lit for Shemini Atzeret. Some people light two candles, while others prefer to light one candle for each member of the family. (Please read Important Information about Candles on page 32.) Remember that the Jewish calendar marks days from sunset to sunset, meaning that on the civil calendar the holidays begin on the previous evening.

Blessing for lighting the festival candles

Baruch Atah, Adonai Eloheinu, Melech ha-olam,
asher kid'shanu b'mitzvotav v'tzivanu l'hadlik ner shel yom tov.

Blessed are You, Lord our God, King of the universe,
who has sanctified us with His commandments
and has commanded us to kindle the light of the festival day.

Blessing for lighting the festival candles on Shabbat
When the candles are lit on a Friday evening,
the blessing is slightly different.

Baruch Atah, Adonai Eloheinu, Melech ha-olam, asher kid'shanu
b'mitzvotav v'tzivanu l'hadlik ner shel Shabot v'shel yom tov.

Blessed are You, Lord our God, King of the universe,
who has sanctified us with His commandments
and has commanded us to kindle the light
of the Sabbath and the festival day.

Yizkor memorial candle

This candle, referred to as *yahrzeit* in Yiddish, is lit in honor of loved ones who have passed away. It may be lit on Shemini Atzeret. It is a good opportunity to think about your departed loved ones, and you may want to say a few words about them or recite a relevant poem or prayer. The *yizkor* ("remember") has enough wax to burn for a minimum of 24 hours and is traditionally lit on certain Jewish holidays as well as on the anniversary of the loved one's death. *Yizkor* memorial candles are lit as a cultural custom rather than as a traditional religious obligation, so they may take any form and be lit in whatever manner is meaningful to you.

Kiddush: the blessing for wine (or grape juice)

Baruch Atah, Adonai Eloheinu, Melech ha-olam, borei p'ri hagafen.

Blessed are You, Lord Our God, King of the universe,
creator of the fruit of the vine.

Ha-Motzi: the blessing for bread

*Baruch Atah, Adonai Eloheinu, Melech ha-olam,
ha-motzi lehem min ha-aretz.*

Blessed are You, Lord our God, King of the universe,
who brings forth bread from the earth.

Shehecheyanu: the blessing of gratitude

The *shehecheyanu* is recited for Shemini Atzeret.

*Baruch Atah, Adonai Eloheinu, Melech ha-olam,
shehecheyanu v'kiyimanu v'higi'anu lazman hazeh.*

Blessed are You, Lord our God, King of the universe,
who has granted us life, sustained us, and enabled us to reach this season.

15. Hanukkah

As winter approaches and the days grow shorter, we look forward to celebrating Hanukkah. This is an eight-day holiday beginning on the 25th day of Kislev – it falls during late November or December on the civil calendar. Its origins lie in ancient celebrations of the winter solstice, when pre-Judean civilizations honored the rebirth of the sun or sun god on this, the day of the year with the least amount of sunlight. Following the winter solstice, the amount of sunlight increases daily through the summer solstice in June.

The stories of Hanukkah are of a military campaign fought to maintain the Jewish way of life and a miracle in which a lamp burned for eight days, though it only contained enough oil to last a single day. Over the years, the focus of this holiday has shifted between these two stories, depending upon the religious and political needs and pressures of the time.

The story of Hanukkah really begins some 170 years prior to the Jewish rebellion and the miracle of the oil. In the year 336 BCE Alexander the Great conquered the Persian empire, becoming the ruler of Syria, Palestine, and Egypt. Greek language and culture spread throughout the region in a process known as Hellenization. (*Hellas* means "Greece" in the Greek language.) Greek culture placed great value on physical beauty and pleasurable activities, making it rather incongruent with traditional Jewish values, which emphasize serving

God, living in accordance with the Torah's commandments, and cherishing spiritual life over physical matters. Alexander the Great made certain allowances for cultural differences among his subjects. The Jewish people of Judea (Palestine) were permitted to maintain their religious and cultural identity at this time – though some readily accepted Greek culture, happy to be released from the restrictions of Jewish life and to enjoy the pleasures of Greek civilization.

Following the death of Alexander the Great in 323 BCE, his empire became divided. At first Judea was part of the Ptolemy dynasty. By about 198 BCE Judea came under control of the Greek Seleucid dynasty, ruled by people commonly referred to as Syrian Greeks. It was a time of relative peace in the region.

In the year 175 BCE Antiochus IV became the king of Syria. In his efforts to strengthen and unify his empire, he demanded that his subjects, including the Jews, follow Greek ways. Hellenization became a powerful and rapidly moving cultural influence. Jews who sought wealth and political power during this prosperous time embraced Greek culture, while Jewish peasants were much more resistant to Hellenism. Antiochus increased taxes on the Jewish people in order to pressure them into abandoning their religion.

Some Jews, typically those in more rural areas, remained fully committed to living traditional Jewish lives. Others continued to practice Judaism but adopted Greek language, clothing, and general culture. A certain segment of the Jewish population, particularly those who aspired to nobility, became fully Hellenized, taking Greek names and no longer practicing Judaism. Some Jewish men underwent a painful procedure designed to make them appear to not be circumcised. In turn, rabbis who were resisting Hellenization called for the circumcision standards to be modified. It was during this time that circumcision changed from cutting only the tip of the foreskin to a much more dramatic procedure – one that could not be masked.

Antiochus became increasingly intolerant of those who continued to practice Judaism. Following several rebellions in Jerusalem, Antiochus completely outlawed Judaism, making it illegal to study the Torah, maintain Jewish dietary laws, perform circumcisions, and engage in other Jewish religious activities. Antiochus ordered a statue of Zeus to be placed in the Second Temple and a pig (a non-kosher animal) to be sacrificed at its altar. He also placed a statue of himself in the Temple and began a program of forcing Jews to bow before this statue.

One day, Syrian Greek soldiers were in the town of Modin to collect taxes and force the residents to worship Greek gods. Mattathias, a rabbi in Modin, refused to participate in a pagan sacrifice. When another Jew stepped forward to make the sacrifice, Mattathias and his sons killed the man, as well as the government official who ordered the sacrifice. Mattathias, his sons, and their followers sought refuge in the nearby mountains. Mattathias died about one year after the revolt began, but his sons, who were known as the Maccabees, continued the fight. They led their poorly-armed rebel forces in a guerilla-style campaign against the highly trained and powerfully armed Syrian troops.

In 165 BCE the Jewish soldiers marched on Jerusalem to reclaim the Temple. The Temple had been defiled – it was filthy and contained Greek idols. The resistance fighters cleaned the Temple. They then lit the Temple's seven-branched eternal light, or *menorah*, though there was only enough oil for it to burn for one day. The miracle of the Hanukkah story is that the Temple *menorah* stayed lit for eight days – long enough for more oil to be prepared. The rededication of the Temple occurred on the 25th day of Kislev.

The rebellion of the Maccabees against the Syrian Greeks can easily be interpreted as the Jewish people fighting for their right to practice their religion or as a revolution against foreign occupiers of their land. But the events surrounding Hanukkah can also be seen as a civil war or stark division between traditional and Hellenized Jews. Hellenized Jews wanted to assimilate into Greek culture in order to gain power, wealth, and acceptance in that society. These aspirations offended the traditional Jews, who viewed the Hellenized Jews as being corrupt and betraying the law of God. The traditional Jews considered Hellenization a major threat to their way of life and were desperate to maintain their customs. It was a time when Jewish individuals had to decide what Judaism meant to them and how to express their beliefs.

Hanukkah is often explained as lasting for eight days to

commemorate the miracle of the oil. However, although the First and Second Book of Maccabees (written within 100 years of the Temple's rededication) detail some of the historical accounts surrounding Hanukkah, neither book mentions the miracle of the oil. They indicate that the rededication celebration of the Temple lasted for eight days because it was modeled after Sukkot, Shemini Atzeret, and Simchat Torah, which together last for eight days. Those holidays could not be celebrated at the Temple earlier that year because it was still occupied by Syrian forces. With the rededication of the Temple came the opportunity for a belated observance of Sukkot, Shemini Atzeret, and Simchat Torah.

The Scroll of Antiochus, most likely written in the second century CE (well after Antiochus's death), does describe the miracle of the oil. The land of Judea was under oppressive Roman rule at the time this scroll was written, and the Jewish people craved hope in their lives. The story of the miracle of the oil encourages hope over despair, reassuring us that God will provide for us and protect us. Shifting the focus of Hanukkah from honoring the Maccabees to honoring God was critical for another reason. Doing so undoubtedly helped the holiday survive the Roman occupation of Judea, since at that time it would have been very dangerous to tell stories of Jews successfully revolting against foreign occupiers.

The miracle of the oil is also described in the Talmud, which barely references the military victory of the Maccabees. One reason for the minimization of the military campaign is that the subsequent history of the Maccabees transformed their dramatic rebellion into a rather minor event. More than 22 years after the Maccabees recaptured the Temple, Simon the Maccabee (a son of Mattathias) succeeded in establishing Judean independence. The Hasmonaean dynasty, named for the Maccabees and their descendants, lasted for a mere 100 years. During that time, the Hasmonaean dynasty actually became Hellenized and even persecuted rabbis. This terrible irony reduced the military victory of the Maccabees to a relatively insignificant footnote in the course of historical events.

The most recognized symbol of Hanukkah is the *menorah*, a candelabrum with nine branches that is more accurately referred to as a *hanukkia*. The *hanukkia* holds eight candles, one for each day of Hanukkah, plus the *shammash*, or "servant" candle, which is used to light the other candles. It is traditional to use an oil lamp for a *hanukkia*, particularly one that uses olive oil as fuel. Most people today use lamps that hold small candles made of wax. (There are also electric lamps, though most modern Orthodox rabbis discourage their use; they are to be employed only if necessary, such as at a nursing home or other location where candles are not permitted.)

On the first night of Hanukkah we place a candle on the far right side of the *hanukkia*. On the second night we place two candles at the rightmost positions. Another candle is added to the left of the previously placed candle for each day of Hanukkah until, on the last day of Hanukkah, there are eight candles in addition to the *shammash*. The *shammash* has a special spot on the *hanukkia*, either above the other candles or off to one side. The candles are lit from left to right, so that the candle representing the first night of Hanukkah is always the last one to be lit.

The candle lighting for Hanukkah begins shortly after sundown – unless it is the Sabbath, when the candles should be lit just prior to sundown. On the first night of Hanukkah it is traditional to recite three blessings: two for the candle lighting, followed by the *shehecheyanu* blessing of gratitude. On the subsequent nights, only the candle-lighting blessings are recited. (These blessings and further instructions for lighting the Hanukkah candles are detailed at the end of this chapter.)

The *hanukkia* symbolizes the miracle of the oil in the Hanukkah story. It also serves as a beacon of light against the darkness of the winter solstice, harkening back to Hanukkah's pagan origins. Some families light a single *hanukkia*, while others have a *hanukkia* for each member of the family. It is customary to light the *hanukkia* next to a window, sharing the light with others and proudly demonstrating that Jewish traditions are observed in the home. Of course, this should only be done if it is safe to have a burning flame at that location. Many people sing "Maoz Tzur" ("Rock of Ages"), a 13th century hymn, after lighting the candles.

The spinning top game called *dreidel* ("to spin" in Yiddish) is a popular activity associated with Hanukkah. There is a tale that this game was invented during the time of Antiochus IV's rule. Because Antiochus had outlawed the practice of Judaism, Jews had to gather in secret for Torah study. They brought *dreidels* with them and would take out the spinning tops whenever Syrian soldiers came near. The soldiers would think that the Jews had gathered for a game, rather than to illegally study the Torah.

Despite this compelling story, the game of *dreidel* may not have existed in ancient times. *Dreidel* was not described in Jewish texts until around the year 1500 CE. It appears to be an adaptation of a game played during the Christmas season in England and Ireland. The game migrated to Germany and became incorporated into Jewish homes.

Dreidel is played as a game of chance. Hanukkah *gelt* (Yiddish for "money") may be used, either in the form of real or chocolate coins. Other items can also be used, such as candy, nuts, poker chips, or small trinkets. Before a player spins the *dreidel*, each player antes one coin (or other object) into the "pot" in the middle of the playing space. The result of the spin is determined by which symbol is facing up when the *dreidel* comes to rest.

Symbols on the Dreidel

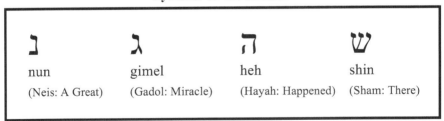

נ	ג	ה	שׁ
nun	gimel	heh	shin
(Neis: A Great)	(Gadol: Miracle)	(Hayah: Happened)	(Sham: There)

If the person who spins gets *nun*, then nothing happens on that turn. *Gimel* means the person wins the entire pot on the table. Half the pot is won when a player gets *heh*. (The number is rounded up when there is an odd number of objects on the table.) *Shin* means the player puts in a coin for that turn. Again, all the players ante before the next player spins the *dreidel*.

The four characters, *nun, gimel, heh,* and *shin* stand for the words *Neis Gadol Hayah Sham*, which translate as: "A Great Miracle Happened

There," referring to the miracle of the oil in the Hanukkah story. *Dreidels* in Israel are slightly different. The letter *pei* (פ) is substituted for *shin*. *Pei* stands for the word *Poh*, meaning "Here." In Israel, then, the saying is: "A Great Miracle Happened Here."

There are other games that can be played using *dreidels*, such as trying to spin the *dreidel* upside-down so that the small handle is in contact with the tabletop. Players can also hold contests to see whose *dreidel* spins the longest or try to knock each other's *dreidels* down as the spinning tops collide.

There are several foods associated with the celebration of Hanukkah. Ashkenazic Jews typically have potato pancakes – *levivot* in Hebrew and *latkes* in Yiddish. Sephardi Jews and Israelis enjoy *sufganiyot*, a kind of doughnut. Both of these foods are fried in oil, in homage to the miracle of the Hanukkah story.

Hanukkah, also called *Hag Ha-Urim* ("Festival of Lights"), is actually a minor holiday on the Jewish calendar. Its great popularity today in the United States and some other countries is a direct result of it falling so close to Christmas, a holiday that is enthusiastically celebrated in the mainstream Christian culture. Hanukkah has become increasingly commercialized in order to "compete" with Christmas, and it is often described – quite inaccurately – as "the Jewish Christmas." While both holidays evolved from ancient pagan observances of the winter solstice and share some common imagery, the religious and cultural meanings of these two holidays are vastly different.

Some Jewish people feel a bit uncomfortable during the winter holiday season, perhaps resulting from a stronger sense of being "different" this time of year. This may be a glimpse into how many Jews may have felt under the influence of Hellenism in Judea, struggling with being a religious minority within the larger, compelling Greek culture. Just as they had to choose for themselves how much they wanted to assimilate into the mainstream, so are we in a position to define our personal and family values within the larger culture of our country. Fortunately, we are able to make these choices freely, a right not afforded to the Jewish people who lived under the rule of Antiochus IV.

It is a great irony that so many Jewish people have chosen to model their celebration of Hanukkah on a holiday from another tradition. After all, Hanukkah is a commemoration of an uprising fought by Jewish people who refused to assimilate into the dominant culture. But in this day and age, some of us find ourselves wishing – on some level – for Hanukkah to be more like Christmas. This is evidenced by the introduction of products such as "Hanukkah bushes," outdoor Hanukkah lights, and Hanukkah-themed party supplies, greeting cards, and gift wrap. The giving of gifts during Hanukkah has also become much more elaborate than in the past. These developments encourage us to indulge in some of the cultural traditions of Christmas and allow us to fit in more comfortably with the dominant society.

Modest gift-giving is a traditional aspect of Hanukkah. In the past, children tended to receive a bit of Hanukkah *gelt* and other small gifts. In the United States and elsewhere, the giving of gifts has become prominent, easily overshadowing the meaning of the holiday. Many Christians are equally upset about the growing emphasis placed on gift-giving during their holy day of Christmas.

Instead of giving extravagant gifts, some families choose to share simple gifts, such as homemade presents, spending time with each other engaged in special activities, or donating to charities instead of purchasing presents for each other. (Searching online will provide many ideas for simple, meaningful gifts.) Alternatively, the number or cost of store-bought gifts can be reasonably limited in order to maintain the integrity of the holiday. One fun tradition is to give children a *dreidel* each year for Hanukkah. They will build quite a collection of different models and styles over the years!

Hanukkah has many compelling themes. As a holiday rooted in ancient observations of the winter solstice, the Festival of Lights celebrates the earth's cycles of lightness and darkness as the seasons change. The light of Hanukkah is a symbol of hope – both for the rebirth of the sun and our ability to live as Jewish people within the dominant Christian culture. The light may also be seen as our inner lights battling against tyranny, as the Maccabees fought against their oppressors. Theirs is a story of an improbable victory, a triumph of the few over the many. Their revolt reminds us that we do not have to fully assimilate into the wider culture, that we are free to follow our own customs and can stand up for our beliefs. The miracle of the oil tells us that we may indeed have plenty even when we fear we do not have enough. Themes of dedication and rededication are prominent in the story of Hanukkah. It is a good opportunity to think about what we would like to dedicate or rededicate ourselves to doing or improving in our lives. Hanukkah is a holiday of great hope and a time to be proud of our cultural traditions.

Hanukkah: Blessings and Candle Lighting Information

Lighting the menorah (hanukkia)

On each night of Hanukkah we light candles on the *hanukkia*, or *menorah*. We light one candle for each night so that there is one candle on the first night, two on the second, three on the third, and so on. In addition to the candles for each night, there is the *shammash*, or "servant" candle, which is used to light the other candles. Candles are placed in the *hanukkia* from right to left, but then lit from left to right so that the last candle lit each night is the one that represents the first day of the holiday.

There are a few different traditions for how to light the candles. Most commonly, we are instructed to light the *shammash*, recite the blessings, and then light the other candles using the flame from the *shammash*. The first two blessings are recited every night of Hanukkah. On the first night only, we also recite the *shehecheyanu* blessing of gratitude.

Remember that the Jewish calendar marks days from sunset to sunset, meaning that on the civil calendar the holidays begin on the previous evening. The *hanukkia* should be lit just before sunset, though many families wait, if necessary, in order to make sure everyone is present for the candle lighting.

Blessings for lighting the Hanukkah candles

Baruch Atah, Adonai Eloheinu, Melech ha-olam,
asher kid'shanu b'mitzvotav v'tzivanu l'hadlik ner shel Hanukkah.

Blessed are You, Lord our God, King of the universe,
who has sanctified us with His commandments and

has commanded us to kindle the lights of Hanukkah.

Baruch Atah, Adonai Eloheinu, Melech ha-olam,
sheh'asah nissim la'avoteinu bayamim hahem bazman hazeh.

Blessed are You, Lord our God, King of the universe,
who wrought miracles for our forefathers in days of old, at this season.

Shehecheyanu: the blessing of gratitude

The *shehechyanu* is recited on the first night of Hanukkah only,
following the two blessings for the Hanukkah candles.

Baruch Atah, Adonai Eloheinu, Melech ha-olam,
shehecheyanu v'kiyimanu v'higi'anu lazman hazeh.

Blessed are You, Lord our God, King of the universe,
who has granted us life, sustained us, and enabled us to reach this season.

16. Tu B'Shevat

There is a story told of a man named Honi, who was taking a walk. He came to an old man planting a carob tree. Honi asked the old man, "Why are you planting this tree? It will take 70 years for it to bear fruit, by which time you will surely be dead!" The old man replied, "That does not matter. Just as my grandfather planted trees for me, so shall I plant for my grandchildren."

Judaism has a long history of honoring trees, as well as nature in general. According to the Bible, we are forbidden from destroying fruit trees, even when attacking an enemy city. Trees are revered for their life-sustaining properties and environmental importance. There is even an old saying that if you are planting a tree and the Messiah arrives, you should finish planting the tree before going to greet the Messiah, for redemption can be found in the act of planting trees.

Tu B'Shevat literally translates as "15th of Shevat," the date on which this holiday is celebrated. This corresponds to late January or February on the civil calendar. Tu B'Shevat is sometimes referred to as the New Year of Trees, and people in times past believed that trees were judged by God on Tu B'Shevat, just as humans were judged on Rosh Ha-Shanah. It was said that on Tu B'Shevat God determined how much fruit the trees would produce in the coming season.

The time of Tu B'Shevat marks the end of the rainy season in the land of Israel. It is time for life to awaken from its winter slumber and for the first flowers and fruits to start forming on the trees. While life is beginning to stir in the land of Israel, more temperate climates are still experiencing winter weather when Tu B'Shevat arrives.

Tu B'Shevat may have evolved from an ancient pagan celebration of the goddess Aherah (also known by the names Astarte and Ishtar), whose symbol was a tree. During Temple times, Tu B'Shevat was a tithing day for fruit farmers, when they paid a certain amount of money based on their fruit trees to help maintain the Temple and its community. After the destruction of the Second Temple, the tradition of tithing ended, and Tu B'Shevat was not widely celebrated for many years. This minor holiday became more popular around the 16th century when Jewish mysticism – *Kabbalah* – flourished. It has also seen a resurgence of interest in recent years with the modern environmental movement and the desire of many people to reconnect with nature.

While describing Tu B'Shevat as a "Jewish Earth Day" or "Jewish Arbor Day" is not exactly inaccurate, these labels don't capture the deeper spiritual meaning of the holiday. Tu B'Shevat is about our relationship with God as much as our relationship with nature. We are told that God expects us to contribute to the harmony of the natural world as responsible stewards of the earth. On Tu B'Shevat we symbolically return to the Garden of Eden, to harmony with nature. We also reconnect with the law of God, for the Bible is often referred to as the Tree of Life.

Neither the Torah nor the Talmud provide specific instructions for observing Tu B'Shevat. Many people choose to celebrate Tu B'Shevat by planting trees, either physically on their own property or in their communities, or through financial contributions to agencies that plant trees. We should also inspect any trees we may have on our property to see if they require care. (If weather conditions do not allow for a proper tree inspection on Tu B'Shevat, make a point of doing this task in early spring.)

For those who live in cooler climates where it is not yet time to plant, this is a good time to start seedlings indoors to transplant outside when spring arrives. These can be tree saplings or plants for a vegetable arden. Some people start indoor gardens or grow alfalfa sprouts, which are ready to eat in only a few days. Many like to plant parsley (either to grow indoors or transplant outside) so it will be ready to harvest for the Pesach *seder* in a couple of months. Parsley grown from seed may have only a few sprigs in time for Passover, but it is still a meaningful way to tie the two holidays together.

Another way of observing Tu B'Shevat is to eat fruits from trees that grow in the land of Israel, such as dates, figs, olives, pomegranates, carobs, and nuts – especially almonds. There are a variety of dishes from Israel and the Middle East that feature fruits and nuts. This is a good time to enjoy fruit preserves made from your garden harvest during the previous season. (Some people specifically make fruit preserves from Sukkot's *etrog* to eat on Tu B'Shevat.) You can also use this occasion to donate money to the poor, particularly to agencies that work to alleviate hunger in the local community, as a way to honor the ancient tithing tradition.

During the 16th century Jewish mystics developed a special *seder* for Tu B'Shevat, with the first written instructions for such a *seder* being published in 1753. The Tu B'Shevat seder incorporates a wide variety of foods grown on trees, images of nature, four mystical spheres of creation, and ten *sefirot* (divine qualities of God) to create a celebratory ritual meal. A Tu B'Shevat *seder haggadah* may be found online and in bookstores with a broad selection of Jewish texts. Or you may want to develop your own Tu B'Shevat *seder* using your personal interpretations of nature and spirituality.

Have a festive table setting for your Tu B'Shevat *seder*. Decorate with flowers, pine cones, stones, other objects from nature, or photos or drawings of the natural world. You may want to use a special plate on which to place the fruits and nuts for the *seder*. A candle with a tree scent can add to the ambiance.

During the course of the *seder*, we drink four cups of wine – just as in the Pesach *seder*. (These should be small cups, as they are enjoyed as part of a ritual meal and not for the purpose of becoming intoxicated.) For Tu B'Shevat the four cups of wine are used to symbolize nature's progression from winter to spring. The first cup of wine is white, reflecting the dormant state of the earth in winter. The second cup is mostly white wine, with a splash of red wine added. The third cup is mostly red wine, with a splash of white. The fourth cup of wine, representing nature in full bloom, is all red. White and red grape juices may be substituted for the wines.

We also eat ten fruits from each of three categories. The first category has inedible outer shells. These shells represent an outer defense that protects the holiness within. Foods from this category may include pomegranates, coconuts, bananas, oranges, grapefruit, walnuts, almonds, pine nuts, chestnuts, hazelnuts, Brazil nuts, pistachios, and pecans. Foods with inedible outer shells correspond to the *sefirah* called kingdom and the sphere of creation called *assiyah*, or "action." This is the simplest level of creation and involves the physical world, intentionally affecting reality by taking action and performing *mitzvot* (commandments or good deeds).

The second category of foods has edible skins but inedible pits that represent impurity. Examples of these are olives, dates, cherries, persimmons, apricots, peaches, plums, loquats, jujubes, and hackberries. Foods with inedible pits are associated with the *sefirah* of loving-kindness and correspond to the sphere of creation *yetzirah*, or "formation." *Yetzirah* is characterized as emotion, prayerfulness, thought, and language. It involves fashioning one thing from another and being creative.

Totally edible fruits (without outer shells or inedible pits) represent purity and holiness. These include foods such as grapes, raisins, figs, apples, pears, raspberries, strawberries, blueberries, carobs, and quinces. While some of these, such as apples, do have seeds inside, they do not contain large pits and so are considered to be in the totally edible category. (The seeds inside may not be desirable, but they are edible.) These fruits denote the *sefirah* of understanding and the world of *beriyah*, or "creation." *Beriyah* involves creating something from nothing and is associated with conceptualization.

The highest *sefirah* is wisdom. It corresponds to the most elevated sphere of creation, *atzilut* – "emanation." This sphere is infinite and immeasurable and is likened to the experience of initial inspiration. This sphere is not represented by foods, for it is beyond the level of the physical. Rather, we try to glimpse *atzilut* by experiencing smells, such as the scents of bay leaves, cloves, or cinnamon.

During the Tu B'Shevat *seder* we symbolically progress through the spiritual spheres, relating these to various fruits and nuts, the natural world, and verses from the Torah. As with the *seder* conducted at Pesach, this *seder* can be adapted to meet your own interests and those of your guests, and it is best to encourage your guests to participate and feel actively engaged. You may, for example, ask them to bring some of the foods needed for the *seder*, artwork depicting nature, poems about trees, relevant quotes from the Torah or Talmud, and other readings about nature and springtime. Some people incorporate songs into their Tu B'Shevat seder or have everyone plant seedlings as part of the celebration.

The following is a most basic framework for conducting a Tu B'Shevat *seder*. Blessings that may be recited as part of the seder are found at the end of this chapter.

1) Drink a cup of white wine.

2) Eat fruits with a hard outer shell, representing
the *sefirah* of kingdom and the sphere of creation
called *assiyah* – the world of doing and making.

3) Drink a cup of white wine with a splash of red.

4) Eat fruits with inedible pits, representing
loving-kindness and *yetzirah* – the world of formation.

5) Drink a cup of wine that is red with some white added –
or half white and half red.

6) Eat completely edible fruits, representing
understanding and *beriyah* – the world of creation.

7) Drink a cup of red wine.

8) Smell sweet spices, such as those from bay leaves, cloves, or cinnamon sticks. This represents wisdom and helps us experience *atzilut*, or emanation. This is likened to being next to God, to being purely in the spiritual realm.

In between each step listed above is an opportunity for explanations of the symbols on the *seder* table, readings, discussions, songs, looking at or creating artwork, or connecting with the themes of Tu B'Shevat in other ways. A meal may be included prior to drinking the fourth cup of wine. This is typically a vegetarian meal and specifically incorporates fruits and nuts into the dishes.

During Tu B'Shevat we recognize our connection to trees, foods that grow on trees, gardening, and farming. We appreciate that being good stewards of the earth is not only good environmental policy, it is also a means of expressing our spiritual selves in relation to the natural world and to God.

Tu B'Shevat: Blessings

The blessings for Tu B'Shevat can accompany a *seder* or be recited on their own.

Kiddush: the blessing for wine (or grape juice)
Baruch Atah, Adonai Eloheinu, Melech ha-olam, borei p'ri hagafen.
Blessed are You, Lord Our God, King of the universe,
creator of the fruit of the vine.

Shehecheyanu: the blessing of gratitude
This blessing may be recited on Tu B'Shevat prior to eating a fruit that has not been enjoyed earlier in the season. In this case, the *shehecheyanu* is recited before *ha-etz* (detailed next).

Baruch Atah, Adonai Eloheinu, Melech ha-olam,
shehecheyanu v'kiyimanu v'higi'anu lazman hazeh.

Blessed are You, Lord our God, King of the universe,
who has granted us life, sustained us, and enabled us to reach this season.

Ha-Etz: the blessing for fruits grown on trees

This blessing may be recited before eating the first fruit of the meal and does not get repeated before eating other fruits during the *seder*.

Baruch Atah, Adonai Eloheinu, Melech ha-olam, borei p'ri ha-etz.

Blessed are You, Lord our God, King of the universe,
creator of the fruit of the tree.

Blessing for smelling prepared spices

Baruch Atah, Adonai Eloheinu, Melech ha-olam,
borei minay vesamim.

Blessed are You, Lord our God, King of the universe,
creator of different kinds of spices.

17. Purim

The joyful, outrageous, and irreverent holiday of Purim is boisterously celebrated on the 14th day of Adar, usually in March on the civil calendar. (If it is a leap year in which there are two months called Adar, Purim is observed during the second Adar.) This is the last holiday of the year on the Jewish calendar. The story of Purim is a farcical tale with little historical evidence to support it. It is, perhaps, the first example of parody in Jewish literature. The Scroll of Esther, often referred to simply as the *Megillah* ("Scroll"), was written between 400 BCE and 300 BCE. It describes the foiling of an evil plot to destroy the Jewish people living in the Persian Empire.

In the story, King Ahasuerus orders his wife, Queen Vashti, to dance naked in front of him and his guests. She refuses to do this and is promptly banished by the king. (In some versions of the story, Queen Vashti is executed.) In search of a new queen, King Ahasuerus invites the maidens of the realm to the capital city, Shushan, so that he can choose which one he will marry. Mordecai, a Jew living in Shushan, brings his younger cousin, Esther, before the king, instructing her not to reveal her Jewish heritage. Ahasuerus is taken by Esther's beauty and selects her as his new queen.

The king's grand vizier is a man named Haman. It is customary for all citizens of the kingdom to kneel or bow before this chief official. One day Mordecai encounters Haman but refuses to bow, stating that Jews bow only before God and not before other people. Haman is outraged and seeks vengeance against all Jews for this offense.

Haman reports to King Ahasuerus that the Jews are not following the law and are therefore a threat to the kingdom and should be killed. The king agrees, and Haman plots to massacre the Jews. As part of his planning, Haman draws lots to choose the date of the pogrom. *Purim* means "lots" in Hebrew, and this is how the holiday got its name.

Mordecai discovers Haman's plot to kill the Jews and shares this information with Esther, begging her to intervene to save their people. No one – not even the queen – is permitted to see the king without an invitation; doing so could result in a death sentence. So it is at great personal risk that Esther approaches the king on her own.

Queen Esther serves alcohol to King Ahasuerus to relax his mood. Once the king is intoxicated, Esther reveals to him that she is Jewish and pleads on behalf of her people to stop Haman's plot. King Ahasuerus decides to call off the massacre and orders Haman to be hanged. Haman dies on the gallows he had prepared for Mordecai, and then Mordecai is appointed to be one of the king's advisors.

The story of Purim is contrived and comical, and the "typical" Jewish experience of life in the Diaspora is turned upside-down. Taking abode in foreign lands, Jewish people throughout history have lived in a delicate balance, vulnerable to the beliefs, whims, and policies of the resident populations and rulers. But in this story, the evil plot is easily toppled and we celebrate a great triumph over anti-Semitism. The joy and elation of Purim hides the insecurity many Jews have felt over the years as a result of being targeted by anti-Semitic attitudes and pogroms.

The party atmosphere during the Purim celebration has some resemblance to Mardi Gras and Carnival. Costumes, role-playing, parody, and poking fun at everyone and everything – even the rabbis and the Torah – are an inherent part of Purim and not found in any other Jewish holiday. The absurdity of the celebration mirrors the absurdity of the Purim story itself.

A common activity is for people to act out the story of Purim in *spiels* ("plays" in Yiddish) filled with satire and mockery. During these performances, the audience makes noise whenever Haman's name is spoken, trying to drown out his name entirely. At the utterance of Haman's name, people may boo, hiss, stomp their feet, blow horns, or sound noisemakers (*grager* in Yiddish, *ra'ashan* in Hebrew).

In addition to putting on plays or skits, people frequently wear masks or dress up during the Purim celebration. Masquerading in anonymity behind our costumes helps us to break free from normal social constraints and to relax and engage in the irreverence of the holiday. Ironically, hiding behind a mask can allow us the freedom to connect to typically guarded aspects of ourselves, as we lose some of our normal inhibitions. Purim masks may be of the characters from the story or of other figures in Jewish history.

Cross-dressing during Purim became popular at the end of the 15th century and is still common today. Indulging in alcohol is acceptable on Purim, and we are told to drink until we can no longer tell the difference between "Cursed be Haman" and "Blessed be Mordecai." Of course, becoming intoxicated (or drinking alcohol at all) is not an actual requirement of Purim, and reckless drunkenness is not tolerated. It would be more accurate to say that consuming alcohol to lighten the mood is encouraged, but becoming drunk is not.

Triangle-shaped cookies called *hamantaschen* ("Haman's pockets" in Yiddish) are the featured food of Purim. They are typically filled with prune preserves or fruit jam. The triangle shape is said to recall that Haman wore a tri-cornered hat. In Italian, these cookies are called *orecchie di Haman* ("Haman's ears"), probably referring to an old tradition of cutting off a criminal's ear prior to execution. *Kreplach*, triangle-shaped dough usually filled with meat or mashed potatoes, is also commonly eaten on Purim.

It is customary to give food – usually fruit, baked goods, and desserts – to family and friends on Purim. We can also provide for the poor through charitable donations of money or food. As part of your observation of Purim, you may consider making a donation to a local food bank, international famine relief organization, or agency that helps the homeless. Assisting others can also take the form of *gemilut hasadim*, or acts of kindness. We can work in our communities to help those who are hungry by volunteering at food banks, soup kitchens, or homeless shelters, or by delivering food to our neighbors or others in need.

We do not light festival candles for Purim. The only blessings associated with Purim are the *kiddish* over the wine and a series of three blessings recited prior to reading the Scroll of Esther. (See the end of this chapter for details on these blessings.)

The origins of Purim are rather unclear, though it may have evolved from an ancient Babylonian new year festival. Babylonian mythology includes characters by the names of Ishtar, Marduk, and Humman. These names are so similar to the names of Esther, Mordecai, and Haman that it appears likely there is a connection between the two traditions. The earliest descriptions for observing Purim instruct us to read the *Megillah*, indicating that this is a formal activity. There is no suggestion of levity associated with Purim until the appearance of the Babylonian Talmud (written between the third and fifth centuries CE), in which we are instructed to drink until we can no longer distinguish between "Blessed by Mordecai" and "Cursed be Haman." Since then, the Purim celebration has become increasingly irreverent, with parodies and carnival atmospheres gaining prevalence over the years.

The story of Purim is not part of the Torah but is found in the Book of Esther, which established Purim as a holiday. Nowhere in the story is God specifically mentioned, a fact that many have interpreted to mean that God was present but hidden, ensuring the pogrom designed by Haman would not come to fruition. In this way, Purim is much different from other holidays that specifically honor God's prominent role in leading and protecting the Jewish people. Some have observed a parallel between God's hidden presence in the Story of Esther and people hiding behind masks during Purim celebrations.

It is easy to consider Purim to be no more than a lighthearted celebration based on a parody written more than 2,000 years ago. But it is much more than that. Just as the masks of Purim disguise ourselves, the festivities of Purim veil deeper meanings and experiences of the holiday. In many ways, the vibrant holiday of Purim is a reflection of ourselves and our relationship to our Jewish heritage.

During Purim celebrations we are able to laugh at ourselves, our traditions, and even at the Torah itself. In a sense, being able to mock the

Torah allows us to accept the Torah more fully and ensure that it is not elevated to the point of being the object of blind faith or idolatry. This mockery can be likened to friendly jesting rather than to teasing out of spite or cruelty. As such, it allows us to get to know the Torah on a different level – as a friend rather than as a servant or child. This experience gives us a distinctive understanding of the nature of the Torah and of Judaism. As a result, we may feel more deeply connected to the Torah and to our culture.

Purim carries particular weight when related to two other Jewish holidays, Yom Kippur and Shavuot. On Purim, we are permitted to act out in ways that are not normally accepted, and doing this gives us an opportunity to reveal aspects of our inner selves that may normally be hidden, both from ourselves and others. This connection to our inner selves feels much different than when we delve into ourselves through quiet meditation on Yom Kippur, the holiday that is most dissimilar to Purim. On Yom Kippur we free ourselves through abstinence; on Purim we free ourselves through indulgence. Yom Kippur is introspective, quiet, and prayerful, while Purim is extroverted, loud, and irreverent. Although these two days appear to be complete opposites of one another, they both afford us the opportunity to connect with our inner selves and explore our thoughts and feelings through the lens of Jewish tradition.

Purim may well be considered a sort of conclusion to Shavuot. According to legend, the Torah was presented to the Israelites at Mount Sinai shortly after they were released from bondage in Egypt. Although they entered into the Covenant with God at that time, agreeing to follow the law of the Torah, they did so with fear and under duress. Now, at Purim, the Torah can be truly accepted by the Jewish people. With the ability to learn, evaluate, befriend, and even mock the Torah, we can say that we embrace it with all of its complexities and paradoxes – as well as our own.

We accept the Torah with all of its wisdom, guidance, inaccuracies, inconsistencies, historical facts, historical fiction, and myths. We acknowledge both our appreciation of and doubts about the Torah. We see that the Torah and the traditions of Judaism are strong enough to accept the mockery of Purim, and we know that they can survive our questions, evaluations, and adaptations as we express what Judaism means to us as individuals living in the world today.

As the final holiday of the year, Purim concludes the annual cycle of Jewish celebrations. Over the course of the year, we have expressed gratitude for the harvest and the natural world, remembered historical events, retold ancient stories, honored the quest for freedom, explored our thoughts and feelings about a variety of topics, evaluated our goals and behaviors, improved our relationships with others, helped to repair the world by aiding those in need, nourished our spirits, spent time with family and friends, mourned losses, and shared joys. It has been a year of celebrating the Jewish holidays and celebrating life!

Blessings for Purim

Kiddush: the blessing for wine (or grape juice)
This blessing may be recited at home or at a Purim party.

Baruch Atah, Adonai Eloheinu, Melech ha-olam, borei p'ri hagafen.

Blessed are You, Lord Our God, King of the universe,
creator of the fruit of the vine.

Blessings for the Scroll of Esther
If listening to the Scroll of Esther (the *Megillah*) being read, there are three traditional blessings, including the *shehecheyanu* blessing of gratitude, to recite prior to the reading:

Baruch Atah, Adonai Eloheinu, Melech ha-olam,
asher kideshanu b'mitzvotav v'tzivanu al mikra megillah.

Blessed are You, Lord our God, King of the universe,
who sanctified us with Your commandments
and commanded us regarding the reading of the *Megillah*.

Baruch Atah, Adonai Eloheinu, Melech ha-olam,
sheh'asah nissim la'avoteinu bayamim hahem bazman hazeh.

Blessed are You, Lord our God, King of the universe,
who wrought miracles for our forefathers in days of old, at this season.

Baruch Atah, Adonai Eloheinu, Melech ha-olam,
shehecheyanu v'kiyimanu v'higi'anu lazman hazeh.

Blessed are You, Lord our God, King of the universe,
who has granted us life, sustained us, and enabled us to reach this season.

Resources and References

Websites

These websites have excellent sections about the Jewish holidays. Along with extensive information, they also list various activities, arts-and-crafts projects, recipes, and other resources. (There are many other websites about Jewish holidays, but these are good places to start.)

www.myjewishlearning.com

www.chabad.org

www.aish.com

Books

These are some helpful books to learn more about the Jewish holidays. I found all of these especially valuable in my own research.

Drucker, M. (1994). *The Family Treasury of Jewish Holidays*. New York, NY: Little, Brown and Company.

Falk, M. (1996). *The Book of Blessings: New Jewish Prayers for Daily Life, the Sabbath, and the New Moon Festival*. New York: HarperCollins.

Kalman, S., Levinrad D., & Hirsch, A. (1992). *Celebrating the Jewish Holidays: Cooking, Crafts, and Traditions*. New York, NY: Crescent Books.

Rush, B. (2001). *The Jewish Year: Celebrating the Holidays*. New York, NY: Stewart, Tabori & Chang.

Scharfstein, S. (1999). *Understanding Jewish Holidays, Historical and Contemporary*. Hoboken, NJ: KTAV Publishing House, Inc.

Steinberg, P. (2007). *Celebrating the Jewish Year*. (Janet Greenstein Potter, Ed.). Philadelphia, PA: The Jewish Publication Society. (Note: This is a three-part series.)

Strassfeld, M. (1985). *The Jewish Holidays: A Guide and Commentary*. New York, NY: HarperCollins.

Glossary and Index

afikomen The broken piece of *matzah* that is hidden during the ritual Pesach *seder*. 26, 30.

aravot (singular: **aravah**) Hebrew: branches from a willow tree. One of the four species (*arba minim*) used during Sukkot. 66, 67.

arba minim Hebrew: the four species. Used during Sukkot. The four species are the *etrog*, *lulav*, *aravot*, and *hadasim*. 66-67.

Aseret Yemei Teshuvah Hebrew: Ten Days of Repentance. The period of time between Rosh Ha-Shanah and Yom Kippur. 52.

Ashkenazi (plural: **Ashkenazim**, adjective: **Ashkenazic**) Jewish person whose ancestors lived in Germany, France, or Eastern Europe. 6, 22, 46, 83.

assiyah The world of doing and making from Kabbalist tradition. 90, 91.

atzilut The world of emanation from Kabbalist tradition. 90-91, 92.

bar mitzvah, bat mitzvah Jewish rite of passage for 13-year-old boys (*bar mitzvah*) and 12-year-old girls (*bat mitzvah*) in which they accept some adult Jewish responsibilities. 44.

beitzah Roasted egg featured on the Pesach *seder* plate. 25.

beriyah The world of creating from Kabbalist tradition. 90, 91.

blintzes Thin pancakes, filled with cheese when eaten at Shavuot. 46.

bourekas Stuffed pastries, filled with cheese when eaten at Shavuot. 46.

b'rakhah Hebrew: blessing. 11.

challah Hebrew: bread. 46, 51, 52, 71.

derash Hebrew: interpretation. In Judaism there is a tradition of *derash* in which we are encouraged to draw our own conclusions regarding our religious beliefs. 4.

Diaspora The dispersion of the Jewish people around the world. 15, 20, 33, 41, 42, 51, 72, 73, 95.

dreidel Spinning top used to play a game of the same name during Hanukkah. 81-83, 84.

etrog Citron that is used symbolically during Sukkot. One of the four species (*arba minim*). 66, 67, 70-71, 89.

gelt Yiddish: money. 82, 84.

gemilut hasadim Acts of kindness. Part of *tikkun olam*, or repairing the world. 8-9, 10, 28, 50, 96.

geshem Prayer for rain recited during the holiday of Shemini Atzeret. 72-73.

grager Yiddish: noisemaker. Used during the Purim celebration to drown out Haman's name. 96.

hadasim Hebrew: branches from a myrtle bush. One of the four species (*arba minim*) used during Sukkot. 66, 67.

haggadah Guidebook for the ritual *seder* meal. Used on Passover and Tu B'Shevat. 27-29, 89.

Hag Ha-Asif Hebrew: The Festival of Ingathering. Another name for Sukkot. 62.

Hag Ha-Aviv Hebrew: The Festival of Spring. Another name for Pesach. 20.

Hag Ha-Katzir Hebrew: The Festival of the Harvest. Another name for Shavuot. 41.

Hag Ha-Matzot Hebrew: The Festival of Unleavened Bread. Another name for Pesach. 20.

Hag Ha-Pesach Hebrew: The Festival of the Paschal Lamb. Another name for Pesach. 20.

Hag Ha-Urim Hebrew: The Festival of Lights. Another name for Hanukkah. 83.

Ha-Hag Hebrew: The Holiday. Another name for Sukkot. 62.

halakhah Jewish law, as described in the Torah and expanded upon in the Talmud. 5-6.

hamantaschen Triangular-shaped cookies with fruit filling that are featured at Purim. 96.

hametz Leavened grains. These include wheat, barley, spelt, rye, and oats. Ashkenazic Jews have added a number of other foods to this list over the years. 22-24, 67-68.

ha-motzi The blessing recited prior to eating bread. 12, 48, 54, 56, 61, 67, 71, 74, 76.

Hanukkah Eight-day holiday celebrated in late fall or early winter. 16, 17, 77-86.

hanukkia Also called a **menorah**. Small candelabrum used at Hanukkah that holds a total of nine candles. 80-81, 85-86.

haroset Sweet apple dish featured on the Pesach *seder* plate. 25

Hasidic Branch of Judaism that focuses on the mystical expression of Judaism, or *Kabbalah*. 5, 28.

Israel Independence Day Recently established holiday celebrated in the spring. 16, 33, 35.

Jerusalem Day Recently established holiday celebrated in the spring. 16, 33, 35-36.

Kabbalah (adjective: **Kabbalist**) The mystical expression of Judaism. 5, 34, 38, 88.

kaddish Prayer for the deceased. 34.

karpas Green vegetable featured on the Pesach *seder* plate. 24-25.

kasher To make utensils and appliances kosher (adhering to Jewish dietary laws) through ritual cleaning. 23.

kiddush The blessing recited prior to drinking wine or grape juice. 31, 48, 54, 56, 61, 67, 70, 74, 76, 92, 99.

kitniyot Legumes. Considered leavened products in Ashkenazic tradition and therefore not kosher for Pesach. 22-23.

knishes Flaky dough pastries, filled with cheese when prepared for Shavuot. 46.

kosher Adhering to Jewish dietary laws. 5, 22, 23, 24, 27, 46, 79.

kreplach Small triangle-shaped dough, usually with a meat or mashed potato filling. 96.

kugel Baked pudding dish, usually made with noodles. 51, 59.

Lag B'Omer Minor holiday that occurs in spring. 16, 38, 40.

latkes Yiddish: pancakes, particularly potato pancakes, commonly eaten during Hanukkah. Called **levivot** in Hebrew. 83.

lulav Hebrew: branch from a palm tree. One of the four species (*arba minim*) used during Sukkot. 66, 67, 70-71.

"Maoz Tzur" "Rock of Ages." A 13th century hymn that is popularly sung during Hanukkah. 81.

maror Bitter herb featured on the Pesach *seder* plate. 24-25.

matzah (plural: **matzot**) Unleavened bread made from wheat and water. Also known as the Bread of Affliction or the Bread of Poverty. Plays an important symbolic role at Pesach. 20, 21, 26, 30, 69.

Megillah Hebrew: Scroll. When used without further details, it refers to the Scroll of Esther, which tells the story of Purim. 94, 97, 99.

menorah Also called a **hanukkia**. Small candelabrum used at Hanukkah that holds a total of nine candles. 80-81, 85-86.

mitzvah (plural: **mitzvot**) Commandment from the Torah; a good deed. 10, 54, 90.

Mizrahi (plural: **Mizrahim**) Jewish person whose ancestors lived continuously in the Middle East and North Africa. 7.

Omer The period of time between Pesach and Shavuot. 37-40, 41.

Oriental Jews Those Jews whose ancestors traveled from the Iberian Peninsula and came to settle in Asia. 7.

Pesach (also referred to as **Passover**) Spring festival celebrating the harvest and freedom from slavery. 14, 15, 16, 19-32, 33, 37, 41, 42, 62, 67-68, 89, 91.

Purim Winter holiday celebrating the fabled foiling of a plot to kill Jews in the ancient Persian empire. 16, 94-100.

ra'ashan Hebrew: noisemaker. Used during the Purim celebration to drown out Haman's name. 96.

Rosh Ha-Shanah The Jewish new year, celebrated in early autumn. 16, 17, 51-56, 57, 63.

Sabbath Also **Shabbat** The day of rest described in the Torah and observed on Saturdays in Jewish tradition. 31, 44, 47, 50, 54, 55, 60, 66, 67, 69-70, 75, 81.

secular Taking place outside of religious institutions. May be associated with religious or spiritual beliefs or may be nonreligious in nature. 1, 6.

seder Ritual meal. There is one for Pesach and another one for Tu B'Shevat. 24-30, 31, 89-93.

sefirah (plural: **sefirot**) Divine quality of God. 38-39, 89-92.

Sephardi (plural: **Sephardim**, adjective: **Sephardic**) Jewish person whose ancestors lived in Spain and Portugal. 6, 7, 22, 25, 83.

shammash Hebrew: servant. Candle used to light all the other candles on the *hanukkia* or *menorah*. 81, 85.

Shavuot Late spring or early summer festival commemorating the harvest and the receiving of the Torah at Mount Sinai. 15, 16, 19, 33, 37,

About the Author

Valerie Toizer Bloom was raised in a humanistic Jewish family. Since having children of her own, she has expanded upon her knowledge of the Jewish holidays and introduced a variety of rituals to her family's celebrations. Feeling connected to her heritage and sharing the richness of it with her children has been a joyful and meaningful experience for her.

Made in the USA
Lexington, KY
10 July 2013